D1397699

UNIVERSITY OF CHICAGO STUDIES IN LIBRARY SCIENCE

A CRITICAL APPROACH TO CHILDREN'S LITERATURE

A CRITICAL APPROACH TO CHILDREN'S LITERATURE

*The Thirty-first Annual Conference
of the Graduate Library School
August 1–3, 1966*

Edited by SARA INNIS FENWICK

THE UNIVERSITY OF CHICAGO PRESS
CHICAGO & LONDON

THE UNIVERSITY OF CHICAGO STUDIES IN LIBRARY SCIENCE

The papers in this volume were published originally in the
LIBRARY QUARTERLY, *January 1967*

THE UNIVERSITY OF CHICAGO PRESS, CHICAGO 60637
The University of Chicago Press, Ltd., London W.C. 1

CONTENTS

v

A CRITICAL APPROACH TO CHILDREN'S LITERATURE

INTRODUCTION

A CONTINUING search for the ingredients of knowledge, understanding, and sensitivity fundamental to serious criticism and interpretation of children's literature led to the designing of a conference titled "The Critical Approach to Children's Literature" in August, 1966. This was the Thirty-first Annual Conference of the Graduate Library School of the University of Chicago, and the papers presented at this conference make up the contents of this publication.

Probably the most important guide since 1953 in the professional criticism of children's literature has been *The Unreluctant Years: A Critical Approach to Children's Literature,* written by Lillian H. Smith, formerly head of the Boys and Girls House of the Toronto Public Library, and published by the American Library Association. It seemed fitting that a conference in this field should pay tribute to the volume that has influenced the education and professional orientation of writers, critics, librarians, and students of children's literature for more than a decade. The subtitle of Miss Smith's book was chosen as the most appropriate title for this conference.

The criticism of children's literature has become a lively art in recent years —in part, because an increasing number of books are being written for children, and in part because there have been drawn into it commentators from many fields of interest. Reflected in the increased volume of reviewing of children's books is a widespread concern, shared by parents and educators, for the quality and validity of children's experiences with literature.

Speakers and participants at this conference brought to the discussions a variety of definitions of children's literature, but the emphasis of the program was upon literature that can provide for children satisfying and worthwhile experiences of joy, inspiration, self-realization, and increased wisdom. Children's literature, then, in the context of these papers, was regarded as a segment of all serious literature, a commentary upon life in dimensions that are meaningful to children.

In a field that has its foundations in several broad areas of scholarship and social process, it was necessary to establish a fairly narrow focus. Without doubt, it would have been profitable to have a symposium on the implications of current learning theories for the child's confrontation with literature; an

1

equally rewarding approach would have been found in an intensive consideration of reading and listening as the most frequent modes of access to literature. It seemed worthwhile, however, to focus our attention upon the literature itself. As has been pointed out by Joseph Wood Krutch, there is need for adults to "bring children to literature" as well as to "bring literature to children." Such an emphasis should not ignore the importance of introducing literature in terms of children's interests and needs, but it should also recognize that overzealous attempts to bring literature to children has resulted in digests, oversimplified versions, and poor films.

The purpose of the program was to widen the knowledge, sharpen the perceptions, and deepen the insights that the participants bring to the critical evaluation and interpretation of children's literature.

The development of bases for a critical approach to literature were considered as first steps, with an opening paper which examined the dimensions of literary criticism and their exercise in the framework of children's reading. The needs of children, developmental as well as environmental, were considered in the following three papers which analyze the psychological significance of children's literature and the sociological setting of reading in the child's world today.

Several selected aspects of children's literature were considered in papers by three authors of books for children and two students of the field. These aspects, while narrowly defined as form, quality, subject, and attitude, are representative of broad types of literature and a variety of interests of children.

Two approaches to evaluation of literature were dealt with by an educator who examined the objective evidence of children's responses to literature and by a reviewer who surveyed the current output of reviewing of children's books.

The final paper interprets the historical role and contemporary responsibility of the critic in the shaping of children's literature.

If it can be granted that a function of a critic is to share new insights and examine relationships that may be unexplored, then it is to be hoped that the discussions brought to life by the authors of these papers will continue and will be extended to other facets of literature for children.

Assistance from the Joseph Fels Foundation in defraying the expenses of the conference is gratefully acknowledged.

SARA INNIS FENWICK

Director of the Conference

CHILDREN'S READING AND ADULTS' VALUES

EDWARD W. ROSENHEIM, JR.

ONCE upon a time there lived a professor of English who had a wife and three sons. (I begin in this fashion not only because we are concerned with children's literature but because I wish to make clear that the following narrative is purely fictional.)

The father had some reason to be pleased with his sons, including the fact that they all seemed to be what are sometimes known as "readers." He viewed with pleasure the fact that their noses, like the parents' noses, often seemed to be in open books. A peace-loving man, he was grateful that their indoor hours were more often spent in reading than in destructive and noisy pastimes. They would, at times, ask him the meaning of various hard words, and he enjoyed the opportunity for modest lexical pontificating. Once in a great while he would allow his own studies to be interrupted and would, rather absent-mindedly, listen to his children telling him what they liked or did not like about certain books and why; but, since he was extremely busy with work on important questions of literary criticism and education, these sessions were very brief, and he soon hastened back to his own labors.

This state of affairs might have continued indefinitely, but one day the father was suddenly invited by certain generous colleagues to do some thinking and talking about children's literature. As the father of children who "read," he cheerfully assumed that some thoughts on the matter would readily come to him, and so he promptly—too promptly —accepted the invitation. And then he sat down to take inventory of what he knew about children's literature—its character, its problems, its opportunities—and abruptly discovered that he knew almost nothing at all. His own childhood reading had become a mere cluster of hazy though affectionate memories. He had frequently listened to an amiable radio program called "Carnival of Books," but the experience had provided no material for significant generalizing. He thought of a few phrases to the effect that books are friends, or new worlds, or frigates bound for far-off lands, but, as he pondered these familiar maxims, his reflections were interrupted by his children, who summoned him to watch the television closeups of the Gemini astronauts being taken aboard an aircraft carrier.

At this point he reached the conclusion that he might best begin by paying some real attention to what his own children were reading. And thus he decided to address himself, more or less systematically, to an inspection and inventory of his children's reading. Here are a few of the things he found out.

All three sons had long squabbled fiercely for possession of the daily newspapers, to which they addressed themselves with the absorption of confirmed addicts. Yet it now became abundantly clear that their attention to these journals was exclusively confined to the sporting news, the comic strips, Ann Landers, and an occasional account of a particularly lurid murder, rape, mutilated corpse, or comparable delicacy.

Beyond this, news, features, editorials, reviews, columns were uniformly neglected.

The reading of one son was largely made up of stories of detection and violence, sporadically relieved by aging, third-rate novels which lay around the house and happened to strike his fancy. He was richly and inevitably familiar with the total James Bond canon, well-versed in Mickey Spillane, and so on. Infrequently he came mysteriously into the possession of a nugget of contemporary pornography, which he read with immense solemnity and no apparent ill effect.

A second son was a Civil War buff of an order to delight the heart of Bruce Catton. His erudition was exclusively confined to American history between the years 1861 and 1865, but within that somewhat limited range it was massive. His father, who was not unfamiliar with pedants, discerned in him the telltale signs of that breed, not only in his willingness to dwell masterfully, if rather tediously, on the tactical minutiae of the Battle of Vicksburg, but in his categorical indifference to all facts and ideas not demonstrably connected with the War between the States. The father, who had hitherto regarded his son's preoccupation as vaguely "broadening," began to suspect that it might be just the opposite.

The reading habits of the third son were, in a way, the most spectacular. Often he would immerse himself so completely in books that he was impervious to all calls to duty—and frequently to meals. What must be noted, however, is that the literary objects of this obsessive attention were exclusively, exhaustively concerned with baseball— the polemical pages of the *Sporting News*, the formidable tables of the rec-

ord books, the imagined exploits of fictional diamond virtuosi, the autobiographies and "how-to" volumes professedly composed by retired major-league titans.

The father contemplated these and similar data with growing uneasiness and self-doubt. "I am," he said, "a student of criticism, and criticism is centrally concerned with artistic excellence; yet excellence seems conspicuously lacking in the literature to which my sons are devoted. I am," he went on, "a college teacher, devoted to the concept of breadth and diversity in the educational process, yet here is reading as narrowly intense as that of the most crabbed scholarly specialist. I am," he thought with further dismay, "a citizen and father, responsibly alert to the terrible challenges and unprecedented opportunities of the modern world, yet here is reading that either evades actuality or presents it in pitiably minute, distorted fragments."

"And yet," he replied to himself, "you are an adult, with adult's values. Your standards and preoccupations, your researches, your critical controversies are quite remote from questions about children's reading. A child's world is not a man's. Children neither need nor seek from literature what adults do. Be satisfied that your children read at all, recognizing that whatever they read stirs their fancy, and most of what they read teaches them something, however slight. Their school, moreover, is exposing them to reading of accepted excellence, their studies are providing diversified encounters with reality. Besides, even if their own leisure reading could be improved, you lack the competence to do the job. Instead of the training of the scholar and critic, the task calls for the specialized insights of psychologists, of librarians, of elementary and secondary educators, of those, in fact, who are willing to suspend their adult values to enter into the needs and circumstances of growing youth."

"But," he in turn retorted to himself, "I cannot believe that questions of good and bad, of artistic awareness, of breadth, of learning, of responsibility—all of which concern adult, professional critics—are alien to the experience of any literate human being. Certainly some of the things that go on in my world have relevance for the reading of my children—none of whom, after all, is very far from the age of the students with whom I do feel competent to deal. And if these things are true, certainly some of the matters that are on the minds of critics can apply to our judgments of children's reading and may even suggest what, if anything, can be done about those judgments. I propose to think—and perhaps even to write—about this."

Accordingly the father sat down in his study and did some thinking—and even some writing. He was, in fact, kind enough to send me a few written remarks, which, with his permission, I am now going to pass along to you.

The word "reading," like the word "literature," is far too broad to be useful for more than a few cheery generalizations, whether we are discussing the reading of adults or of children. Certainly one may begin with one familiar, necessary distinction—which can be simply, if controversially, expressed as the difference between reading conducted for its own sake and reading conducted for the sake of something else, usually learning or training. In the first category would fall the reading of what is sometimes called "imaginative literature," including poetry, drama, fiction, certain kinds of essays and speculations; in the second category would fall all other books, juvenile and adult, which seek to tell us how things actually are or have been or ought to be. And I would think the problem of judging the excellence, the "worthwhileness" of books in the second category—whether books on history or social questions or science or geography or religion or conduct or art itself—would simply involve determining the intelligibility, attractiveness, persuasiveness, importance, and usefulness of whatever could be learned from them. It may be very difficult to write such books—and difficult, too, to motivate children in reading them—but to assess and justify their role in the total reading experience seems relatively simple.

It is with the other type of reading, the imaginative, the reading that is pursued for its own sake, that the problems of justification and judgment become very troublesome indeed. They are, in fact, so controversial that they are precisely the questions to which critics and teachers of literature have characteristically addressed themselves during these recent decades, which some people have characterized as an Age of Criticism. Yet these questions produce answers, though never definitive ones, and they produce certain beliefs about literature, again never universally accepted, and these answers and beliefs do have a bearing on children's reading as well as adults'.

It is, in the first place, characteristic—though not by any means inevitable—that today's critic recognize that the greatest power of imaginative literature, in its various kinds, is to yield particular satisfactions—that is, unabashedly to assert that such literature is primarily read for pleasure. This may seem an unexciting, if debatable, commonplace, but I can assure you that, if so, it has only recently become one. I have dismal evidence that in classrooms—and even in recent printed curricular materials—the child's reading of a lyric poem or fantasy or even a comic short story is immediately followed by some such initial question as, "What does the work teach us?" or "What do we learn about so-and-so?"

Yet the primacy of pleasure as an end in reading is now quite widely accepted, and we have indeed gone further and asked some searching questions about the nature and sources of that pleasure. And because those sources properly lie in only two places—the written work before the reader and the mind of the reader himself—we have been led to concentrate upon that unique, immediate encounter between book and reader, largely, and quite deliberately, neglecting such peripheral matters as the biography of the author, the circumstances under which the book was composed, its reputation, or—as I've already suggested—its "lesson." And, in consequence, we find ourselves driven to think, not primarily about authors and subject matters and "reading" generally, but about specific books and their readers—what goes on in books, what goes on in the people, young and old, who read them.

Our thinking has prompted many of us to feel that there are pleasures, even "literary" pleasures, of many kinds. We recognize that certain species of work yield certain species of satisfaction. Beyond this, we have begun to suspect that there are degrees of pleasure that are largely determined by the degree of affirmative intellectual energy a reader

is willing to invest. There are, we feel, the satisfactions, legitimate enough but rather flabby, that come only from a sort of effortless recognition of what is reassuringly and comfortably familiar, whether that familiarity is bred by authentic experience or by previous reading as in the case of "series" books. There are the satisfactions of what I like to think of as "easy fantasy"—often represented by the kind of escape-cum-identification literature one found in so many boys' books in my youth, in which, against a background of sport or youthful society that offered no challenge to the imagination, youngsters like myself enjoyed a more glamorous and triumphant life than their own. There are, again, the transient titillations afforded by flamboyant and minimally credible writings which exploit the violent or exotic or prurient or sentimental. The appeal of such work is assuredly the province of the psychologist, whose findings tend to remove these experiences from the area of intellectual—or at least aesthetic—satisfaction.

All these are pleasures, each authentic enough, frequently entirely respectable, that somehow fall short of the pleasures that can be achieved by reading, the pleasures proper to true humanistic experience. And I use the word "humanistic" because, in this kind of pleasure, we inevitably make active exercise of our uniquely human gifts—the gifts of apprehension, of imagination, of discrimination, of relationship, of judgment. The humanistic satisfactions are not those of temporary, uncritical surrender (much as we like to speak of "enchantment") but of sustained, active encounter—the kind of encounter that makes a Holden Caulfield want to telephone Old Thomas Hardy or causes a Mary Poppins to exist so vitally in the imaginations of her young admirers that, as many did, they reject her unconvincing embodiment on the movie screen.

Reading to achieve these satisfactions involves, obviously, an energetic act of the intellect—and the capacity for such an act requires cultivation which is certainly not that of mere literacy. It means, to put it bluntly, that we cannot have it two ways: if reading is to yield its deepest, most permanent, most humane satisfactions for our children, then the mere gesture of "reading," mere uncritical pleasure in reading, is not quite enough. If we are concerned with reading for maximum satisfaction, we parents and teachers must be prepared to devise strategies, provide help, and—above all—make judgments about our children's books.

And these judgments are, of course, difficult to make. But I would suggest that, if my concept of the most satisfying reading is a correct one, we do not bother inordinately with questions such as, "Is this a great book?" Or a wholesome one. Or an up-to-date one. Or an informative one. Or even a "broadening" one. The questions I would ask would tend to be: Will this book call into play my child's imagination? Will it invite the exercise of genuine compassion or humor or even irony? Will it exploit his capacity for being curious? Will its language challenge his awareness of rhythms and structures? Will its characters and events call for—and even strengthen—his understanding of human motives and circumstances, of causes and effects? And will it provide him with a joy that is, in some part, the joy of achievement, of understanding, of triumphant encounter with the new?

All this may appear to put a some-what pretentious light on the problem. Yet, after all, most of the special human satisfactions do require planning and training in their cultivation. Even the deepest, most appropriate satisfactions from sport—either of the participating or spectator variety—are achieved through training and practice in execution or experienced, sophisticated appreciation. And if we grant only that the satisfactions of imaginative literature are equally rich and permanent, then it seems reasonable that we think about their cultivation with equal care and responsibility. And thus, to accept the "pleasure principle" is anything but an evasion of the duty to think about reading. It is, on the contrary, to accept the obligation to think resourcefully and carefully and devotedly in the interests of that motive which, for most parents, assumes the highest priority, the nature and magnitude of our children's happiness.

A second preoccupation of many critics in recent years has been with the question of literary kinds or genres—a problem that, at first glance, may seem rather lifeless and remote from the questions that should be concerning us. Yet I think it has some consequences for our thinking about children's literature. For many years, booklists, anthologies, and even literature courses and curriculums tended to classify works according to gross form—poems, plays, and novels—and, within such groups, according to "topic" or "subject matter." Thus a typical anthology of poems or stories for young people might bear such headings as "Nature," "Foreign Lands," "Sport," "Other Times," "Here and Now," "Adventure," "The World of Science," or whatnot. In short, classification was preceded by certain judgments—frequently not entirely accurate

—as to what a work was "about"—that is, into which very general category of human experience its contents might be pigeonholed. But the tendency of most modern criticism, especially in its educational implications, is to suggest that there are far more significant categories than these—that the structure and tone and, in particular, the peculiar effect of a literary work offer far more revealing modes for its classification. We have, that is, addressed ourselves (with, I admit, sometimes highly conflicting answers) to such questions as what is a lyric poem, a tragedy, a comedy, a naturalistic novel, an absurd play, an adventure tale, a satire—and we have recognized that such reliable old guides as subject matter or historical period have not proved very useful. For we ask, not "What will the reader learn about?" but "What kind of experience is he invited to undergo?"

The consequence of this for the high school and college classroom is easy to see. It is plain that *Oedipus* and *Othello* bear strong relationships, despite the 1,900 years that separate their composition; it is plain that *Gulliver's Travels* and *Catch-22* have powerful affinities, despite the disparity of their "topics"; it is plain that *Huckleberry Finn* can afford closer comparison with the *Odyssey* than it can with *Penrod*, despite the fact that it might be lumped with the latter under some such heading as "Books about Boys." In short, we have become increasingly sophisticated about distinctions and relationships between literary kinds—and this has had profound effects both on criticism and pedagogy.

I would suggest, therefore, that in thinking about children's reading we relax somewhat about "topics." The boy whose consuming passion is the Civil War need not confine himself to century-old reprints of *Harper's Magazine* or special publications of *American Heritage*, but is likely, on the contrary, to find his way to biographies of Lincoln and Lee and the stories of Ida Tarbell and *The Red Badge of Courage* and even perhaps to "When Lilacs Last in the Dooryard Bloomed." The youthful baseball aficionado will quite likely come, at his own rate, to the comedy of Ring Lardner, the unique achievement of Mark Harris's "Bang the Drum Slowly," the high art of Malamud's *The Natural*. The James Bond addict can be led on to Eric Ambler's intricate plotting and thence to Graham Greene's reflective "entertainments" and thence, I venture to say, to Stevenson and even to Melville.

Thus, beneath the apparent uniformity of "subject-matter" labels, there lies diversity of a far more important sort. No topic is intrinsically more "worthwhile" than another; no topic is either a guarantee of, or a bar to, the sort of satisfactions I have mentioned previously. They can serve us as singularly useful devices by which to engage interest and by which, too, to exploit the happy diversity of literary experiences which, on the surface, they tend to obscure. In effect, if a youngster is entirely concerned with reading about the Civil War, we should view it neither apprehensively as "obsessive" nor smugly as "educational." Instead, I should think we can view it as a natural and immensely promising channel, leading to a permanently rewarding diversity of humanistic encounters.

A third question that has interested many critics in recent years might be put as follows. Are there basic themes or "motifs" whose expression and recognition in written and spoken literature help to explain the timeless appeal of certain kinds of stories and poems? I am talking here about something a little more fundamental than even such formulas as boy-meets-girl or the tale of revenge or the "whodunit."

The inquiries of such anthropologists as Frazer, such psychologists as Jung, and such scholar-critics as Northrop Frye have pointed to the fact that some of man's most basic questions and doubts and hypothetical answers tend to take form in recurrent literary patterns—or archetypes, as they are often called.

To take an example from a field that interests me: one persuasive scholar has been able to talk about the nature of satire, even in its most sophisticated forms, by tracing its origins to certain tribal rituals, directed against hostile forces, and has gone even further back to various informal, minimally artful attempts to achieve, through extemporaneous curses, the same magical effects.[1] The work of another scholar, Philip Young, has noted the recurrence of such literary themes as the suspension of time (in stories like that of Rip Van Winkle or the many "time machines") or the stories of kings' daughters who rescue their lovers from wrathful fathers (such as the tale of Pocahontas).[2] Not content with noting the origins of some of these literary motifs in folk literature, he has applied psychoanalytic insights into the reasons for their persistence—the needs and wor-

ries and wishes that thus find embodiment in mythic form.

In their particulars, many of these approaches still call for refinement. But I am of the opinion that they are bringing us substantially closer than ever before to answering questions we have previously evaded or answered peremptorily and unsatisfactorily. They are questions, that is, that concern the unchanging appeal of certain basic kinds of literary construction.

I am not certain how thoroughly the implications of these studies have been explored with respect to children's literature—although it is plain that many of these motifs find their most uncomplicated and manifest embodiment in myths and fairy stories and folktales. What, for the moment, concerns me is their possible significance for that nagging problem, the problem that is variously defined as engagement or motivation.

I have, to be honest, been somewhat concerned with the manner in which I have discovered this problem is being handled in various curricular study centers and similar agencies designed to deal with children's reading in the schools. I have found, for example, that the principle of familiarity—of comfortable recognition—has been rather overworked in many places. It is argued that the child cannot be expected to show interest in the unfamiliar and even that literature should make no demands upon him that transcend the literal limits of his own experience. This has an odd effect on what we judge to be "suitable." If a story involves a city, let it be a city he knows—or knows a great deal about. If a poem involves a bird, let it be a native bird (exit nightingale). If a play is to be read, by all means let it be a play of the here and now.

[1] Robert C. Elliott, *The Power of Satire: Magic, Ritual, Art* (Princeton, N.J.: Princeton University Press, 1960).

[2] Philip C. Young, "Fallen from Time: The Mythic Rip Van Winkle," *Kenyon Review*, **22** (Autumn, 1960), 547–73, and "The Mother of Us All: Pocohontas Reconsidered," *Kenyon Review*, **24** (Summer, 1962), 391–415.

Such a principle seems to me to be a pretty frail one. I believe it is frail in practice. Most teachers of English composition know that because a child owns a dog or has visited a farm there is no guarantee that he will write readily or enthusiastically about "My Dog" or "The Farm." And most teachers of English and concerned parents soon recognize that the familiar is at best a partial handle on children's literary enthusiasm—doubtless for the very simple reason that the commonplace is the commonplace and therefore the most unexciting object to the imagination.

And one need not be a very subtle aesthetic theorist to sense the difficulties of a lopsided emphasis upon the familiar. Whether we quote Aristotle's dictum concerning the mixture of the probable and the marvelous in successful literature or Marianne Moore's lines about "imaginary gardens with real toads in them," the principle seems pretty clear. Effective imaginative literature is an amalgam of the new and strange—what taxes credulity and complacency with what is somehow believable, authentic, and immediate. And I should argue that if the balance is to be tipped it must be tipped in the direction of novelty, of the alien and challenging. For all genuinely memorable literary experience is, in some measure, an initiation into the previously unknown, and the overworked reviewer's phrase to the effect that after reading such and such one is "never quite the same" is, quite literally, a criterion that may be applied to the judgment of any literary work.

The word "romantic" is today a very unfashionable one, but it is the thrust toward romance, or at least toward the imaginative, that outruns experienced actuality and that, today as much as ever, remains a major weapon against sameness and stagnation. This is heartbreakingly apparent, for example, even in the street gangs of our cities, whose ritual and nomenclature and professed structure and self-image, it has been proven, far exceed the sordid actualities of their operations. The same phenomenon is present in the almost universal manifestations of Walter Mittyism, among the old and young, wherever the imagination is invoked in the struggle against the too familiar. Mittyism may be professionally explained as escapism or the buttressing of the *amour propre* or as protest, but, whatever its ends, the means plainly involve the enlistment of the imagination in combat against familiar reality.

I am rejecting the temptation to say that new, unfamiliar kinds of reading should be encouraged in order to "stretch" the imagination and to "broaden horizons." I happen to believe that there's a good deal of truth (and some danger) in this position, but the question that immediately concerns me is that of engagement and motivation. And in this context I am simply urging that we can overdo the matter of familiarity—if it leads us to neglect the appeal of whatever strains against the boundaries of the commonplace.

But it is obvious, as I have suggested, that novelty must be balanced against the reassuring sensation of knowing where one is, that the totally alien lacks both intelligibility and consequence for any reader. As critics have always recognized, we can become engaged in literature only when it is, in some sense, "credible," when it lays claim, in some fashion, on our sense of reality. Many writers—including writers of children's literature—have responded to this requirement by attempting to invest the familiar with the romantic, to exploit, as it were, the potential magic that is latent in everyday reality; or they seek to introduce the strange and incredible into the midst of the commonplace. This last, of course, is what has been done triumphantly in such works as *Mary Poppins* or *Stuart Little* or *Doctor Dolittle.* And the former kinds of things are worthily attempted in the familiar efforts to exploit the "romance of coal" or the "miracle of oatmeal" or "the wonderful story of sewage disposal," largely for didactic reasons.

Awareness of motifs or archetypes, however, suggests that the recognizable to which we respond is not necessarily a matter of times, places, and institutions but of the basic needs we feel, questions we ask, answers we find—of the instinctive, universal challenge of the journey, tension of the conflict, the covert wish that magic mingle with reality, the complex drives of affection, the complex fears of death.

I am aware that talk of this kind breeds discomfort of sorts among parents and those who are devoted to children, professionally or otherwise. Because we love and cherish the childlike, we naturally seek to preserve it and to translate even children's reading into terms that reject many of the adult "facts of life" as somehow corrupting. Talk of conflict and love and birth and death, of tension and terror and doubt, and even of driving curiosity seems hostile to the image some people foster of "children's literature" as a world unsullied by the adult vision of reality—as a monument to wholesome naïveté. I am, in fact, tempted to speculate that the fatuous admiration professed by some sophisticated adults for the idyllic surroundings, the allegedly benign humor, the unworldly wisdom of *The Wizard of Oz* or *Alice* or *Winnie-the-Pooh* is not so much what it pretends to be—a recognition of "adult" excellences in "children's" books—as a wistful gesture of longing to recover an irretrievable, happy innocence.

It is certainly possible to view children's books as instruments for the confirmation of childishness—to rejoice in whatever preserves the guileless and ingenuous. I suspect that to do so is, in itself, an evocation of impossible magic. The child is, indeed, in all his growing faculties, the father of the man; the faculty of imagination is not a childlike gift but a faculty capable of robust, complex development. As I have mentioned archetypes, let me say that no archetype is more compelling and dangerous than that of the fall of our first ancestors, for it points to the most uncomfortable yet inevitable fact about the human condition. This fact is that the acquisition of wisdom is the loss of innocence. The fact has received ingenious evasions. From Plato, through Wordsworth, through Hugh Walpole's neglected, lovely, subversive *Golden Scarecrow* to the pubert-directed reassurances of *The Catcher in the Rye,* we have been told that the innocence of childhood somehow preserves a greater wisdom and virtue than the sagacity of adults.

Such doctrines, however attractive they may be, are mystical rather than humanistic. For the humanist, above all else, takes into account the realities of the human condition. And those realities do not lead us into a beautiful, passionless realm but are compounded of hope and fear, of doubt and reassurance, of need and the fulfilment of need. It is in encounter with these human facts that we develop uniquely human values; and they are the values we seek to develop in and share with our children.

What I have been trying to say is, first, that the problem of "engagement" or motivation can only be met by a judicious blending of what is novel and unfamiliar with what is real and significant. And, second, I have suggested that the latter component is to be achieved, not necessarily through those overtly familiar sights and sounds and people and places we identify as what the child "knows," but through the more basic recognitions of experienced needs and satisfactions, doubts and curiosities and preoccupations.

There is a story by Saki that may help me clarify my point. It is called "The Toys of Peace." In it two well-meaning, pacifically inclined parents are induced to substitute for their children's toy soldiers a set of new playthings, in which military installations and personnel are replaced by a model city hall, municipal disposal plant, figures of various worthy civic servants, and the like. The children are given these toys; but the parents return, after some absence, to discover that through the children's ingenuity the city hall has been converted into a fort, the garbage plant into another fort, and the street-sweepers, health officials, and doctors and nurses have been assigned the role of soldiers on both sides of a fierce and bloody imagined conflict. Leaving aside whatever motive was in the strange mind of Saki, the story still serves my purpose. The "realistic," familiar, but dreary figures of civic virtue are rejected in place of the more remote, less recognizable, more "romantic" figures of war. Yet, in that act, is a gesture not only toward romance but toward reality as well, toward a state of contest and dissension and uncertainty which has,

in a sense, a greater authenticity than does the image of a benevolent and orderly universe.

The tendency of what I have been saying is toward the recognition of certain principles that may transcend such notions as "maturity" and "reading readiness" and "suitability" and the like. It is designed to suggest that, if we don't fatuously accept children's literature as primarily a safe, sane, antiseptic device for the preservation of childishness, its most fundamental appeals are the appeals of all effective literature —it exploits our urge toward novelty as it exploits, too, our insistence on a human actuality that is an amalgam of glory and squalor, certainty and anxiety, nobility and baseness, or, for that matter "good guys" and indubitably bad ones. And this belief, it seems to me, moves to close the gap between adults' values and children's reading. It suggests that we do not seek substitutes, in children's books, for the most cherished elements in the best adult books. It suggests the folly of "approving" books that are mere superficial mirrors of what we think children are or ought to be, mere superficial representations of a children's world or what it ought to be. For the highest pleasures of literature to which I have already referred—whether in adults' reading or children's—combine the urgency and authenticity of life as we know it with the excitement and wonder of life as it may yet be known.

This is why I believe that "great" children's literature, if I may use that tired term, is simply great literature. It is no accident, nor is it mere clinical curiosity, that accounts for the critics' interest in Greek myths or in *Robinson Crusoe* or *Treasure Island* or *Just So Stories* or even, for that matter, in the perennial fairy or folktales. The sources of adult curiosity, adult humor, adult suspense, adult terror, adult pity are exploited by the writers of such books with an art comparable to that of any author for any audience. If I happen to have been talking about what are called "classics," I do not wish to be construed as believing that the existence of classics is central to any belief I have about reading by children or adults; the appetite for reading, in old and young, far outruns the capacity of a few men to produce books of transparently permanent greatness. But it seems only sensible that, when the satisfactions literature can offer are superlatively afforded by a certain, limited number of books, we should seek to experience these works. It seems equally sensible that our experience with these books should reveal, in some measure, the satisfaction that many other books are capable of affording— the satisfactions that young and old alike should seek from reading.

As great books differ from good books in degree rather than kind, so too, I think, successful children's books differ from successful adult books in degree rather than in kind. Obviously this view follows from a belief that, with respect to the faculties of understanding and the gift of appreciation, young human beings differ from older ones in degree rather than kind. Granted that youthful powers of attention and concentration are limited and thus raise real and difficult questions for us, our concern with these questions must not deter us from the recognition that neither attention nor concentration are the faculties to which literature ultimately addresses itself in children or adults.

The point of all this (for the problem that confronted the hypothetical professor confronts us all today) seems rather clear. What I have been trying to say expresses my belief that the judgment of children's literature—and all the adult efforts that proceed from that judgment—must be conducted without condescension, without turning one's adult collar in an effort to define and enforce values that are somehow uniquely juvenile. On the contrary, it seems to me that the proper satisfactions of reading, even in the newly literate child—even, indeed, in the nonliterate, story-listening child—provide a robust affirmation of our common humanity, our capacity, whether we are young or old, to understand and to be moved by and to gather to ourselves the products of the creative imagination.

As I say these things I am deeply conscious of circumstances at this moment in history which may qualify my views and chasten my high hopes. Talk about rich literary experience may seem appallingly ironic in the context of the massive phenomena of minimal literacy, minimal ability to understand and communicate. A teacher of English cannot today carry on glibly about literary values without agonizing awareness of the presence of culturally deprived youngsters for whom literature can be expected to have little meaning, since such words as "father" and "bedtime" and even "breakfast" have themselves virtually no meaning. Here are children who seem, indeed, to be separated in kind rather than degree from the hypothetical young readers with whom I began these remarks.

To the crushing, compelling challenge posed by such youngsters (as well as, I might add, by those ostensibly more privileged youngsters in whom parental apathy, television, and aggressive vulgarity have likewise engendered a brand of cultural privation) we must respond with whatever is relevant of our experience, our love, and our concern. Even in these instances, however, though we respond with total flexibility and undogmatic resourcefulness to problems of minimal communication, the imagination is an indispensable ally, and the awaking of the imagination, a relevant province of art. For there are windows to be opened, and when they are open, they must reveal a vista of more than squalor and sameness and spiritual poverty.

It is common today to insist on a distinction between mere communication, including written communication, and literary art, whether or not that art is actually practiced in writing. Because, in practical and perhaps theoretical terms, some mode of communication is always antecedent to art, communication may well demand priority in much of our educational thinking, just as minimal questions of material well-being demand priority over questions of total well-being.

But, though we distinguish communication from art and concentrate upon the former in all its urgency, all its changes, all its opportunities, the nature and stature of literary art and its satisfactions suffer no change. Though in our folly we neglect literary art, though in our haste we seek substitutes for it, though in our complacency or cruelty we discourage access to it for many of our fellowmen, art and its power remain unchanged.

And this may provide a glimmer of insight into the dilemma of the professor with which I began. Nothing he feels about his children should alter what he feels about literature—and his feelings about literature should obviously prompt him to relax about some things in his children's reading and to query others. For I choose to believe that my professor is a humanist. The realm of the humanist (and by this time I hope it is clear that the values I have been describing are, in my view, humanistic) is the realm of what has been created by human wisdom and imagination, work that has achieved final form, work that waits to be known and savored and remembered for the unique satisfactions it provides. And so it is that a belief in the value of reading leads to a concern, not primarily for what is desirable or appropriate, what is suitable or profitable, what is hard or easy, what can be or ought to be, but for what is *here*—here to be encountered, here to be understood, here to be responded to, here to be rejoiced in.

PSYCHOLOGICAL SIGNIFICANCE OF CHILDREN'S LITERATURE

JACQUELYN SANDERS

EVERY author has his own view of life and of his responsibility as an author; therefore, each work of literature has its own psychological significance. For example, a James Baldwin who says that the function of an author is "to describe things which other people are too busy to describe"[1] is likely to create a literature that has psychological significance quite different from that of an Emily Dickinson who writes, "there is no frigate like a book to take us lands away,"[2] or that of a Tolstoi who says "art is a human activity having for its purpose the transmission to others of the highest and best feelings to which men have risen."[3]

This diversity is as wide in literature written for children as it is in that intended for adults. The question, then, is which of these many significances are the most appropriate for children. Let me, therefore, direct my remarks to certain psychological considerations that are important in determining this.

We must, of course, first ask what are the outstanding characteristics of children? What most markedly differentiates them from adults is that they are not grown and they are growing. As the child grows, he strives to master both an outer world that is continually expanding and an inner world of emotions that are often tumultuous. In both of these realms there are many experiences to be fathomed, from "why does it rain?" to "why do we cry?" As the child fathoms them he gains strength from doing so. There are external demands he must learn to meet, from the expectations of his principal to those of his peers, and internal needs he must learn to satisfy, from hunger to anger. As he successfully fulfils these demands and needs, he grows stronger. Literature can be of value in helping the child cope with and master those problems of importance in his life—be it what to do on a rainy afternoon, how to play a new game, or how to manage anger at one's mother.

We know that the existence of a body of literature represents one of the highest achievements of man, and it is by this means that the discoveries of one man can be passed on to another, miles and years away from him. Some children know this, in their own terms, and expect literature to offer valuable knowledge. Other children have very different, at times very negative, expectations. No matter what the expectations, the selection of literature for children should be such that this message is conveyed. If the child can feel that what he is reading is of importance to him; if he can by his reading gain mastery of an act that he wishes to accomplish, a fact that he is pleased to know, or the understanding of an emotion that has been disturbing him, then the message has been conveyed; and he

[1] James Baldwin, *Nobody Knows My Name* (New York: Dial Press, 1961), p. 153.

[2] Emily Dickinson, "There Is No Frigate Like a Book," in *The Complete Poems of Emily Dickinson* (Boston: Little, Brown & Co., 1924), p. 53.

[3] Leo Tolstoi, *What Is Art?* (New York: Thomas Y. Crowell Co., 1899), p. 57.

has gained from the insights and knowledge of the writer.

To guarantee that the child psychologically experiences literature as a useful tool, the first books that he reads are of crucial importance. In many series of readers this aspect has been overlooked; the learning of the mechanics of reading has been emphasized leaving the content often shallow, occasionally even inane. Fortunately there has been a decided change in regard to content, and a number of interesting readers are now available. The danger in methods that put major emphasis on the mechanics is that the social and psychological value of reading may be drowned. There are children who find with the cues that have been given them that they have a useful tool: they can read that it is cornflakes, not Wheaties, on the breakfast table; they know what Batman is saying to Robin. However, there are others who do not find their way to such delights by themselves.

As a member of the staff of the University of Chicago's Orthogenic School, I had the opportunity of watching some children with severe emotional problems learn to read. Their beginning readers were not the conventional ones. A boy of nine went from a preprimer to the *New York Times* in five months by way of a book called *The 26 Letters*.[4] Though very bright, he had failed first grade twice. For reasons that pertained to his psychology, the changeability of the pronounciation of the letters presented the greatest problem. Therefore, a book that directly investigated this mystery was the book that could provide him with the greatest possible mastery.

[4] Oscar Ogg, *The 26 Letters* (New York: Thomas Y. Crowell Co., 1961).

A seven-year-old boy was suddenly able to read, though no one had attempted to teach him. His texts were the signs he passed; his teacher, whoever would read them to him. Signs warned of dangers and provided controls; knowing what they said enabled him to better protect his life. Thus the full emphasis in his learning was on reading as a tool of mastery. The emphasis on skills was only the casual remark of an adult or the instructions of a teacher to another child.

A third boy learned to read by writing swear words to his counselor. Thus the printed word for him was of value in the mastery of his emotions.

All this is, of course, not news to the reading teacher who has often taught children to read from their own stories. Psychologically, this technique is successful because it guarantees that the issues in the stories are of importance to the child. Being able to read about important things is in itself a mastery over them and, thereby, a demonstration that reading is valuable.

I am not, however, suggesting that the first literature for children be written by children. I am suggesting that it is of great importance—perhaps even greater than that of the words being easy to recognize—that this first literature be of the essence of children's literature: meaningful to the child in his mastery of life. If it be of the outer life, it should be a life that concerns him, neither too pure nor impure; if it be of his inner life, it should be of emotions, both positive and negative, that are related to his own.

Such choice of subject matter guarantees the interest of the child and at least that degree of mastery derived from being able to read about what one considers important. However, it does not guarantee good children's literature. How the subject matter is dealt with, the direction pointed to for mastery, is of critical importance. For example, some of the old fairy tales or Bible stories are fascinating to children because they deal with aggressive and negative traits of human beings and indicate ways of coping with them. Some of these methods are obvious and harsh. The dire fate of jealous siblings, for example, is a clear warning to repress jealousy. These fairly simple tales, sometimes directly and sometimes symbolically, tell of the basic issues of life and how they may be handled.

In considering literature for children we must then ask: first, is the subject matter really of the child's sphere of interest; second, is the subject matter presented in a way that is manageable and conducive to a meaningful experience; and, third, what solutions are made available.

When dealing with children there is a very dangerous tendency to oversimplify and to avoid areas that are unpleasant or difficult. This often derives from too much emphasis on their smallness and lack of ability, and not enough emphasis on their growth and acquiring ability. This tendency can negate the very essence of the value of literature to children, for it can lead to an omission of those things that are of the greatest importance. For instance, the discussion of menstruation in *The Long Secret*[5] is a unique instance in fiction for this age group in spite of its importance. Instead of children's literature being the stairway to knowledge of the adult world and guide to mastery, these tendencies emphasize the difference between adults and children and

[5] Louise Fitzhugh, *The Long Secret* (New York: Harper & Row, 1965).

increase the child's feeling that adults wish to hide knowledge rather than to convey it.

When Maria Montessori advocated the use of china dishes for her little children, she did so because she believed that if they had only unbreakable dishes they would have no reason to be careful. However, she did not leave them with broken dishes. China was difficult for her little ones—her answer was not to avoid it, or to just give it to them, but to teach them how to use it. Areas of life that are difficult, like china, if avoided will not be understood; if simply presented will only be badly handled; but a valuable service can be rendered if these areas are presented together with help in learning how to cope with them. If children are treated with respect, they are more likely to act respectfully. If they are given tin cups because they are so clumsy, they are more likely to be clumsy, but if they are given crystal so they can have beauty, they are more likely to act beautiful. If we give them intelligent reading matter they are more likely to act intelligent.

Certain types of children's literature bring to mind the so-called adult movies. Just as such a designation of movies means, in other words, "sex," the designation "children's literature" means, in other words, "no sex." While children are not interested in adult love or sex from an adult point of view, they certainly are interested in their own bodies, including their sex, and adult love and sex from a child's point of view. However, the general books of information for children are sadly lacking in this area. I have not yet found a children's encyclopedia in which I could find the names of the genitalia. Many of the books on science and anatomy simply ignore these parts as well as the exterior organs of the excretory system. Yet these are the words that children generally want most to look up in the encyclopedias and dictionaries.

The message that this omission psychologically conveys is of more concern than the fact that an opportunity is here missed of giving the child desired and valuable information. When a child looks for this information and cannot find it, he must feel that adults do not want children to know about sex, since the books they write for children do not tell about it.

One boy provided a warning with regard to the oversimplification mentioned earlier. When this boy had finally begun to understand what happens in the process of conception, he explained why he had never understood the explanations that had been given him. When he had been told that the seed of the father united with the egg of the mother, he had always visualized the seed and egg with which he was most familiar—a vegetable seed and a chicken egg. Here, as often happens, oversimplification had led to distortion. It seems better to use the accurate name with children; while the scientific name might not increase understanding of a concept too difficult for a child, it would not give an erroneous idea and would not impede understanding when the child matured emotionally and intellectually enough to comprehend.

In other areas difficult to deal with, neither the classic authors nor the comic-strip authors have avoided emotional content that might be difficult or unpleasant. Some of our thoughtful contemporaries are writing of such things. *Shadow of a Bull*[6] is the story

of a Spanish boy expected to follow in the steps of his father, a famed bull fighter. It tells about death, violence, and cowardice—none of which is easy or pleasant, all of which are of the greatest importance.

When we look at literature of psychological interest, we must ask the second important question. Ford Madox Ford said, "Only two classes of books are of universal appeal: the very best and the very worst."[7] The secret of the appeal is the universality of the feelings described; what makes the difference is how they are described. The two aspects of appeal I would like to discuss are the presentation of the subject matter and the solutions offered.

The first question to be asked in considering the presentation is whether it in itself is manageable for the child. There are some general issues that influence this, regardless of subject matter. If, for instance, the language is incomprehensible, the child will not be able to cope with the subject matter. Similarly, if the material is presented in such a way as to arouse a great deal of anxiety, the child will not be able to cope with the subject. The extent to which a particular piece of writing evokes anxiety has to be related not only to its psychological implications but also to the craft of the writer. For the well-being of the child, the danger lies in depicting a situation with either much more or much less anxiety related to it than is actually reasonable. Ghost stories, for instance, dealing as they do with common fears of the dark, might be told with such vivid exaggeration that they increase such fears rather than help in the mastery of them.

[6] Maia Wojciechowska, *Shadow of a Bull* (New York: Atheneum Publishers, 1964).

[7] Ford Madox Ford, *Joseph Conrad, A Personal Remembrance* (Boston: Little, Brown & Co., 1924), p. 184.

There are certain issues that do arouse, in themselves, a great deal of anxiety. Some of these are simply not suitable for presentation to children—an example might be the using up of the earth's resources. However, there are many such issues that are suitable for children—such as that of conflict. Since a story is not life, some very difficult issues can be dealt with through fiction without creating the anxiety that they do in real life. In this respect fantasy is a method of presentation that has a great advantage, because events that are obviously unreal or very distant do not have as great an emotional impact as those that appear closer to home and therefore more possible. For the child who can differentiate fantasy from reality, the man from Planet X or the Trojan War are not so scary as the chicken pox or a fight with one's mother. However, if the anxiety-producing aspects in fantasy are overemphasized, this advantage is lost.

The second important question in regard to presentation is related to that which the child perceives as reality. Most fictional writing contains some kind of reality: for instance, the factual reality such as is found in historical novels, stories of children in other lands, and science fiction. Obviously, this should be accurate. There is another kind, an emotional reality, that it is equally important to draw accurately since it is perceived by the reader as reality. I refer especially to such things as how people act toward each other and within themselves. This kind of reality exists even in fantasy. The way animals behave toward each other and toward people is very important to children. The behavior of the bird in Oscar Wilde's *Happy Prince* was significant for its love and loyalty. Though the child will know that birds and statues do not talk to each other, he might very well come to believe that kindness engenders love.

When we consider reality in fiction, an exaggeration of the implications of the statements initially quoted might explain two tendencies often found. In the very valid desire of a Dickinson to have literature be that which raises one above misery and reflects the happy life, the unpleasant parts of human interaction may be overlooked. In the equally valid desire of a Baldwin not to overlook such things, the more pleasant aspects of life may be neglected.

The danger in either of these tendencies is that, if carried too far, a distorted picture is presented. If the child perceives them as reality, the story that depicts people as all happy and kind and the one that depicts them as all stupid and angry are equally misinforming. Unintentional as it may be, giving a child misinformation about life cannot help him deal with it better.

Each of these tendencies fills an important psychological function when taken in the appropriate dose. Children as well as adults enjoy the expression in fantasy of both their positive and negative wishes. Literature that provides either of these is certainly providing some of the tools of mastery. The issue that I am here concerned with involves that which the child believes to be a true picture of life and human nature. When the hero of the story is supposed to be an ordinary boy or girl who might live next door, a child might deeply believe that the story tells how life is.

In addition to this reality providing information for the child of how life is, it can also be perceived as a presentation of how life should be. Again, each of the above-mentioned tendencies has its assets and its dangers. If people are depicted as having only positive emotions the child might by contrast feel himself bad and be dissatisfied with himself and all his relationships; or he might strive and dream for a similar unrealistic situation; or he might recognize what it is and stop reading such a foolish book. At the opposite extreme, depicting people as predominately negative presents undesirable models for behavior.

Whether particular behavior tends to be considered desirable or undesirable is often determined by the attitude of the author. In any fairy tale the king who does not treat his subjects well is a bad king; being powerful is good. A children's biography of the late President Kennedy portrayed the family relationships as being fraught with competitiveness. The author described this as highly desirable and part of the reason for the success of the Kennedys. When we consider the likelihood of the behavior depicted being accepted as model behavior, we must ask ourselves if this is the model we wish to present to children.

This last question brings us to the third area of our consideration: that of solutions offered.

Tolstoi's statement that it is the obligation of the author to point out the best ways of coping with life is pertinent here. Since it directly presents the kind of situations children need to cope with daily, the story of an ordinary family deserves major attention. It is reassuring and, therefore, entertaining and ego-building for children to discover that others have emotions similar to their own. Children's horizons can be broadened by reading of other ways to cope with life, other enjoyments that are possible, and bits

of information hitherto unknown. Carolyn Haywood's *Little Eddie*[8] describes emotions familiar to young children and, at the same time, is a horizon-opener. Eddie is a plausible little boy, striving for the possible, encountering obstacles, and managing to overcome them in ways that are often ingenious though not necessarily brilliant. From the height of a little boy such as Eddie, this might well be considered the "highest and best feelings." When, for example, a little girl gets a discarded printing press minutes before Eddie arrives to pick it up, and, despite his disappointment and anger, he does not seek revenge—this is a high achievement. When Eddie then contrives to be able to use the press almost as much as if it were his own, this is truly a best solution.

In discussing solutions offered, I would not like to overlook the great body of classic literature that has offered very definite solutions. For one reason or another, many of these are considered unsuitable as written for use with children; therefore, they are abridged and rewritten. Most such tales have a particular message. Shakespeare made his opinions very clear, but they do not seem so clear in the simplified versions of his plots. If the child cannot understand the original words of a classic, likely as not the theme is not understandable either.

When Bible stories are changed so as to make them less frightening (and in the process lose their moral), they become a negation of a piece of literature that is important to a great many people. Recently I had occasion to compare two children's versions of the story of Noah and the Ark. One stayed

[8] Carolyn Haywood, *Little Eddie* (New York: William Morrow & Co., 1947).

quite close to the biblical version and used biblical language: the flood came because people were bad. The moral was: be good so that you will be one of those saved. The other was a poetical version that gave no reason for the sudden descent of the waters; after they had subsided everyone went home: evidently the flood had done no damage. While I believe that there are better reasons than fear of a flood for people to act decently, it is, perhaps, a better reason than none. Mankind still seems to need some controls, and if these are not the kind of controls those who create children's literature advocate, I do not believe that it is psychologically constructive to destroy such controls for those who do advocate them.

To return then to what fiction can offer to children: the author who emphasizes too much the transcendence of misery might show the "highest and best feelings" without any indication of how to achieve them other than in fantasy. The author who emphasizes too much the problems of daily life might never give any indication of ways to resolve them.

When we find a book like *Harriet the Spy*[9] which makes a noteworthy attempt to deal with many difficult problems, we must ask, "How are they resolved?" and "Will this make it easier for a child to deal with such problems?" For example, describing certain difficult family relationships that are often avoided in children's stories may hold the child's interest, but such descriptions are not necessarily of value if they go no further than describing the child's point of view. If a parental argument is enacted behind closed doors so that the child hears only parts of it, it is intriguing; however, if no further cues are given in the novel as to how the child might cope with it, an excellent opportunity is being missed.

When a method of coping is presented, we must ask if the manner of dealing with the problem is desirable in terms of the child's well-being. Spying presents a distorted picture and so does not really satisfy the curiosity that motivates the spying. I am, therefore, not convinced that Harriet's continuing to spy at the end of this book is a very desirable solution.

To present a problem without indicating the existence of a plausible solution provides the possibility of a certain degree of mastery: that which comes from being able to read about the problem; that which comes from knowing that others recognize or even have the same problem; and that which comes from being able to reduce the intensity of the conflict causing the problem by providing this outlet. Reading about violence might well permit one to keep his violence in check; however, the statement of a problem without any resolution carries with it the danger of intensifying it by appearing to present it as a desirable model for behavior.

At the Orthogenic School, we worked with a boy of fifteen who was fascinated by war. He would read exciting war stories, going over and over the violent parts with his level of interest and fascination remaining the same. When we gave him and read with him *The Cruel Sea*,[10] it became an important factor in influencing his view of war. The book describes how men coped with war, its

---

[9] Louise Fitzhugh, *Harriet the Spy* (New York: Harper & Row, 1964).

[10] Nicholas Monsarrat, *The Cruel Sea* (New York: Alfred A. Knopf, Inc., 1951).

challenge and its horror. Since the men had human emotions, both negative and positive, the boy could identify with them and share the pleasure of their glory; he could also learn from them the price of such glory in war. The solutions that these men struggled to find were both possible and noble. The boy could read about war, yet not be encouraged to think that war is a good solution.

I have suggested that, in looking at children's literature, we ask: first, is the content of interest and importance to the child, so that he knows it is really his? Second, is this content presented in such a way that it is manageable for the child, makes life more manageable, and provides models of behavior that are useful and desirable? And, third, are solutions offered in the resolution of the drama, and, if so, are these solutions feasible and constructive? If the

answers to these questions are *yes,* then the literature has provided the child with most important aids in mastery.

There are, fortunately, those authors who feel a responsibility and believe, as Tolstoi, that "art is a human activity having as its purpose the transmission to others of the highest and best feelings to which men have risen."[11] Some authors assume responsibility for struggling toward the resolution of the basic conflicts of humanity and presenting in their art form the struggle and resolution. The author of children's literature must concentrate on those conflicts that are of the child's world. The best authors are the best psychologists. They provide, through their writings, deep insight into human nature and, thereby, a powerful tool for better living and growing.

[11] Leo Tolstoi, *op. cit.*, p. 57.

A PSYCHOLOGICAL BASIS FOR JUDGING CHILDREN'S
LITERATURE DEALING WITH NATURE
AND SCIENCE

LUITGARD WUNDHEILER

THIS discussion will be concerned with two problems: the child's view of nature and the purposes of the literature dealing with the subject. As regards the first, we may begin with a statement that is perhaps a truism: namely, that the child's mode of thought and therefore his view of the world, including nature, is unobjective and unscientific. But this only says what the child's view of nature is not rather than what it is. In order to be able to describe the child's view of nature we must first deal with the question: what is the child's mode of perception?

Children perceive the world in terms of their emotions rather than in an objective manner. Objective properties of things, such as size, shape, or color, are submerged in the emotional meaning of the object and emerge as isolable perceptual dimensions only slowly in the child's life. The emotional meaning of an object is at first the only meaning that is perceived by the child. An example of this is the infant who may be totally oblivious of extreme noises like the siren of the fire truck and is hardly aware of drastic changes in his environment like a move to a new home, but he becomes lively when he sees and hears his mother enter the room because he anticipates nursing. In Church's words, "developmentally . . . meanings precede objects in perception."[1]

At the age when the child becomes interested in nature or certain objects in nature, such as plants and animals and clouds—that is, perhaps at the age of three or four—he is of course able to recognize objective properties of things to some extent. But his emerging objective perception is still strongly influenced by his emotions. (As a matter of fact, to some extent our perception remains under the influence of the emotions as long as we live. What changes is the degree to which this is so.) In the course of a person's life, objective perception slowly gains the upper hand, and we use it more and more often to correct our emotionally tinged perception.

What does it mean that the child at about age three or four perceives nature and interprets his perception in terms of his emotions? The question may be answered by way of an example. The child often sees faces in the clouds. As he knows that his mother's facial expressions have something to do with her feelings about him or Daddy or the ring of the doorbell, and therefore may signify what she may or may not do for him and with him, he concludes that this must also be true of the clouds and that this is what the faces of the clouds mean. In other words, he attributes feelings and intentions to the clouds as he does to his mother. Or he may see a tree sway in the wind and hear it moan, and he concludes that the tree must be sad. For the child, this sort of percep-

[1] Joseph Church, *Language and the Discovery of Reality: A Developmental Psychology of Cognition* (New York: Random House, 1961), p. 5.

tion is extremely compelling. When he sees a face in a cloud or hears a tree "moan" he has no choice but to conclude that the trees and the clouds have feelings. As adults, we may also sometimes see faces in clouds, but at the same time we are aware that what we see is not a real face but a product of our imagination. The child does not have this choice. When he sees a face in a cloud and hears a tree moan, he cannot help but conclude that a tree and a cloud are living beings and have feelings like his. He is forced to this conclusion because nothing in his experience tells him otherwise; that is, nothing in his experience has made him doubt his emotional perception. The question arises: why is there nothing in the child's experience that tells him otherwise.

Here, Piaget[2] comes to our aid. According to him, the child's way of perceiving the world and interpreting his perception is not only determined by his emotions but also by his cognitive development. When we as adults see faces in the clouds, our perception also is determined by our emotions, but our past experience and our knowledge and way of thinking help us correct our emotional perception. The child's mode of thought and experience is different from ours. Piaget calls the child's mode of thought and experience egocentric and realistic. By "egocentric" he does not mean what is often meant by it— that the child is selfish; he means that the child is incapable of any point of view other than his own. By "realistic" he does not mean that the child's mode of thought corresponds more closely to objective reality than ours but, rather,

that the child attributes to his images and feelings the same status in regard to reality as he does to objects.

Let us return once more to the faces of the clouds and the moaning of the trees in order to illustrate. When a child sees a face in a cloud and believes that the cloud must be a living being, he attributes reality to something that is no more than an image or, you might say, a product of his imagination. This is what Piaget calls the realism of the child. When a child believes that a tree must feel sad because he hears it make a sound that reminds him of a sigh, he does so because he is unable to conceive ways of existence different from his own. This is what Piaget calls the egocentricity of the child.

So much for the definition of the terms "realism" and "egocentricity" as used by Piaget. In order to show whence the child's realistic and egocentric modes of thought and experience arise, we may use one example from Piaget and two from my own observations. Piaget[3] describes how at a certain stage of development the child tends to believe that he can magically influence the clouds, in other words, that the clouds move where he pleases. Piaget makes much of this example because it illustrates the child's egocentric world view. The universe, including the clouds, is believed by the child to rotate around him—the clouds move as the child moves. Let us stop to think where this belief comes from. It comes, of course, from a sensory experience. The child does indeed experience that the clouds move when he moves. That this movement is only an apparent movement he does not realize until much

[2] Jean Piaget, *The Child's Conception of the World* (London: Kegan Paul, Trench, Trubner & Co., 1929).

[3] Jean Piaget, *The Child's Conception of Physical Causality* (London: Kegan Paul, Trench, Trubner & Co., 1930), p. 62.

later because it is very difficult to understand. He has to understand, among other things, that another child moving in the opposite direction believes that the clouds move with him. Objective understanding involves taking the other child's statements about it just as seriously as his own. In short, the child's belief that the clouds move with him is derived from a sensory experience uncorrected by reflection or a more relativistic point of view.

During the course of the last year, I have been engaged in some research in connection with this problem of egocentricity in children and how it is reflected in their views of nature. The following two examples are observations made during this year. One question asked children is, "Do plants feel bad when they are thirsty?" And if the answer was in the affirmative, they were asked, "How do they show it?" Young children up until the age of seven tend to say that plants do indeed feel bad or unhappy when they are thirsty and that they show it by looking sad. Then a little later, when the children are more sophisticated, they will say that plants show that they are unhappy when they are thirsty by drooping their leaves. Still later a highly interesting statement is quite common. The children tend to continue to say, "Yes, plants do feel unhappy when they are thirsty." But then, when asked, "How do they show it?" they will say something like: "Their leaves droop, but I guess that only means that they need water. It doesn't necessarily mean that they are unhappy about it."

This sequence of three answers reflects a development from an entirely egocentric view of nature to a less egocentric view. When a child says, "A plant is unhappy when it is thirsty, and

I know it because it looks sad," he says in effect: "Since the plant looks sad to me, it must feel sad when it is thirsty." Next, when the child says, "The plant feels sad when it is thirsty, and I know it because its leaves droop," he shows a recognition of some difference between himself and the plant. The plant has leaves and no face; therefore, the child says that the plant expresses unhappiness with its leaves. At the same time, the child maintains his egocentricity insofar as he continues to attribute his own emotions to the plant. Finally, when the child says, "Drooping leaves do not necessarily express unhappiness, although it makes the plant look sad to me," he clearly recognizes differences between the plant and himself. What he is saying is: "The plant looks sad to me, but maybe I am different from the plant, and what looks like sadness to me may not be sadness to the plant." This sort of statement ushers in the end of egocentricity as a mode of thinking and the beginning of objective, scientific thinking.

Finally, I have heard many children say that plants can "feel" the sun and that they can "prove" it because hasn't everybody seen plants turn toward the sun? They attribute a connection between conscious feeling and movement to the plant because they are aware of such a connection in themselves. Their egocentric mode of thinking prevents them from considering the possibility that a plant might turn toward the sun for other reasons than conscious desire for warmth and light. In the last two examples, as well as in the one from Piaget, it should be clear that children's views of nature are derived from sensory experiences. In all these examples, children were trying to explain to themselves something that they had observed, that is, seen or heard. When adults say children are so imaginative that they think that plants can feel and think, they are usually only revealing their ignorance of the child's mode of experience. The reason that the child attributes feelings to plants is not that he is so imaginative that he can make it up but that his mode of experience is realistic and egocentric. The child's thought in these matters are fantasy only in the sense that they do not correspond to reality, not in the sense that they are made up, at least not from the child's point of view.

If one looks at children's books on nature, it becomes apparent that most authors have educational purposes, if not explicitly, certainly implicitly. The second part of this paper will be concerned with the question of how children learn. It is my contention that children learn mostly by playing. If this is so, it would follow that if we want children to read, and especially if we want them to read instructive books, the books will have to subserve play. Before giving examples of books that do precisely that, a few words about play are in order.

Usually when we use the word "play" we take it for granted that what children do is play. Yet, when we define the word, we usually define it in adult terms. That is, people will define it, for example, by contrasting it with work, which is, supposedly, what adults do; or they will contrast it with making money or with being serious. Play, supposedly, is not serious, is not work, and has no importance in the money-making world. This definition of play is, of course, quite incorrect. Rather than a definition of play, it can be considered a sad commentary on this society and how unchild-oriented it is despite its claims to the contrary.

For a good definition of play we may turn to Erikson, who has deepened our understanding of children more than most psychologists. According to him, "play is the infantile form of the human ability to deal with experience by creating model situations and to master reality by experiment and planning."[4] As an example we think of a boy who experiments with an adult role by playing pilot, or a girl who experiments with the maternal role by playing with dolls. Or think of the child who tries to master the painful experience of sibling rivalry in doll play.

There are innumerable examples. For the purpose of this paper, however, Erikson's words should be exemplified in terms of the specific area of play with which we are concerned here, that is, play with objects in nature, such as plants and animals and clouds. As we have seen above, objects in nature are considered by the child to be living beings like himself. For this reason he can use them for certain purposes for which no other playthings can be used equally well. In my experience children have used natural objects for two purposes: (1) they assign human roles to them, and (2) they use them to explore the human body and master anxieties connected with it. As regards the first purpose, the child can use natural objects in order to act out with them what may be too dangerous or too painful or too difficult to act out in reality. The child who plays with and takes care of pets or plants often does exactly this. For him, the plant he waters or the animal he feeds often are friends—or enemies, as the case may be. He can assign human roles to plants or animals more easily than to toys, even dolls, because

[4] Erik H. Erikson, *Childhood and Society* (New York: W. Norton & Co., 1950), p. 195.

plants and animals are like human beings in that they are alive, and yet they are sufficiently different to give the child's activity the aura of play, that is, in Erikson's terms, of experiment and planning rather than reality.

I observed one boy who was afraid of his father because his father was big and strong, and he felt himself small and helpless by comparison. In an effort to deal with his fear, he planted two plants, a big one and a small one, and he watered the small one regularly and thoroughly and the big one rarely and sparingly until the small plant had become as strong and healthy as the big one. Although this was a disturbed boy, his was one of the more typical childhood conflicts, so it may be useful to examine what this boy did. He transferred his conflict to the plants so that he could master in play what he could not master in reality.

This example was chosen because it illustrates the difference between play with toys and play with nature. When a child plays with toys, he is in control. When he plays with nature, he is up against a part of reality whose laws he has to learn lest he be frustrated and disappointed. This boy had to learn what amount of water is good for a plant and what amount is insufficient. Also, unless he wanted to starve the big plant to death, he had to find out what minimal amount of water is still sufficient for a plant to live on but at the same time insufficient for growth. Yet, despite the necessity to meet the demands of reality, play with nature remains play. If plants do not react as the child wishes, the shock is dampened because he knows that it is only plants he failed to master and not himself or Mommy or Daddy. On the other hand, if he achieves mastery in nature, the triumph is more lasting than mastery over

toys can ever be because his play partakes of reality.

As regards the second purpose of play with natural objects, namely, that the child can use them in order to explore his body, it is well to remember that the small child's first plaything is his own body. He plays with his hands and feet by the hour and is, of course, learning important things at the same time. It is by playing with his body that he gets a feel for his body and that he begins to differentiate between his body and that of his mother and thereby discovers himself. As he gets older, his main focus of interest is still his own body, but his interest shifts from the body as a thing or part-things (such as his hands and feet) to body processes, like growth, digestion, or sex. When this shift occurs, the child can no longer play with his own body to satisfy his curiosity. No form of play with one's body can answer questions like: what are the forces of growth, or how do they operate? And while children explore their own and other children's sex organs, they explore the functions of these organs first in plants and animals, long before they themselves reach sexual maturity. This is where objects in nature are helpful. One can learn about growth and sex and the beginning of life and other urgent problems by playing with and exploring plants and animals.

What has been said about play should help to elucidate the statement that, if we want children to read, children's books should subserve play. Children want books that give them the information they need in order to use objects in play. In regard to objects in nature, this means that children want to know what acts will have what consequences. Unless they know that, play with objects in nature will not lead to mastery but to defeat. If a plant dies as a consequence of the child's ignorance rather than because he has planned it so as part of his play, he will feel defeated. On the other hand, if a plant grows because a child has taken care of it, he will feel reassured in regard to his own physical as well as intellectual and emotional growth.

There is not time to give an extensive overview of children's books dealing with nature. A few examples of the best will be mentioned to show how they inform the child without stifling him with factual details or difficult concepts he is not able to understand. Some of the very best books have been written by Millicent Selsam. Many of her titles have the word "play" in them: *Play with Seeds*,[5] *Play with Plants*,[6] and *Play with Trees*[7] are some of them. In her books she gives children hundreds of things to do, and all of them demonstrate to children what happens as a consequence of what. In other words, these books give children the information they need in order to plan and experiment on their level.

Of course, not every form of plan and experiment is a form of play. Erikson says that in play the child masters reality by experiment and planning; in other words, only those plans and experiments that help the child master reality are play.

To illustrate what this means in regard to play with nature, let us recall how children use natural objects in order to deal with some of the anxieties related to their bodies. When a child grows a plant in order to find reassurance concerning his own growth, he creates what Erikson calls a "model situa-

[5] New York: William Morrow & Co., 1957.

[6] New York: William Morrow & Co., 1949.

[7] New York: William Morrow & Co., 1950.

tion"; that is, he does not play with his own body but with a plant, and the plant becomes a model for the child's body. To play with his own body or that of his parents or siblings may at times be full of dangers; to play with plants instead helps the child master these dangers in situations that are only models for the real situations.

Mrs. Selsam deals in her books with precisely those processes in plants that are most interesting to the child because they also go on in himself. We could refer to processes like growth or the intake and digestion of food and water, to mention only the most important ones. She describes magnificent and very simple experiments which deal with questions like: what happens to a radish seed when water gets inside it? What parts of a plant need light? What happens when a plant does not get enough warmth? To repeat: these questions are interesting to children because they, too, need water, warmth, and light. Therefore, by doing these experiments the child learns about himself.

While the questions Mrs. Selsam raises are of personal interest to the child, she never anthropomorphizes. This seems important because if one does, one destroys the model character of the situation which the child creates in play. A model must be different from the object it is intended to elucidate and illustrate. Another important point is that Mrs. Selsam never goes beyond the conclusions the child can draw from the observations he himself can make. This is important because children trust their sensory experiences more than the logic of grown-ups; and, if one cannot get along without grown-ups even in play, then very little is accomplished in play.

Another strength of Mrs. Selsam's books is her use of language. She avoids two equally serious, although opposite, pitfalls: she never talks down to the child, and she never uses sophisticated scientific jargon. Her language is very simple, and yet everything she says is absolutely accurate and free from over-simplifications. This is important because not only the content of a book but also its style conveys a message.

Mrs. Selsam's message, as conveyed by her style, is respect for children without overtaxing their abilities. As an example, in her book *Play with Plants* she introduces experiments. To design an experiment is not an easy task, as everyone who has ever tried his hand at science knows. Without going into the more complicated details of the question of how to design an experiment, Mrs. Selsam handles the most basic requirements as follows. First, she gives a concrete example; she describes how to set up an experiment to find out if seeds need warmth to grow. She says, "If you want to prove that seeds need warmth to grow, you grow some seeds in a warm place and compare them with another set in a cold place." Then she goes on to state a general rule for experimental design without one single complicated word and without oversimplification.

This is how she puts it: "Remember that no matter what you want to prove, you should make one part of the experiment where something is present, another part where that something is absent."[8] This says everything that needs to be said, and yet scientific terms like "equal conditions" or "independent and dependent variable" or phrases like "all conditions but one must be held con-

stant" are avoided. This is not to say that the most complicated experiments in physics can be described in the same simple language. But it is one of the virtues of Mrs. Selsam's book that the language is always appropriate not only to the level of the child but also to the degree of difficulty of the experiment she introduces.

There are, of course, other good books on natural objects and forces. There is, for example, Illa Podendorf's excellent book *101 Science Experiments*.[9] Since this paper has been limited almost entirely to the animate part of nature, justice cannot be done to her book, which deals mostly with natural forces like heat and electricity and inanimate substances like air and water. But it is appropriate to raise one question. In my experience many children do not consider air an inanimate substance or magnetism an inanimate force. Children may consider air a living substance because it is life-giving and believe that magnets are alive because anything that exerts a force or causes motion seems alive to a child. There seem to be only very few books that deal with this childish conviction intelligently. Instead, they take it for granted that children will accept the concept of a purely mechanical force. Illa Podendorf deals with this issue in a very subtle way, but not explicitly. It may be useful to elaborate on this question in an attempt to make explicit what is implied throughout her book.

Let us use Einstein as an example. In 1949 he wrote some autobiographical notes as an introduction to a book about him called *Albert Einstein, Philosopher-Scientist*.[10] There he relates an experi-

---

[8] P. 41.

[9] New York: Grosset & Dunlap, 1960.

[10] Ed. Paul Schilpp (Evanston, Ill.: Library of Living Philosophers, 1949).

ence he had as a five-year-old boy which was such that he could not integrate it into the conceptual system he had at that age. Consequently, it created in him the feeling that his conceptual system had to be revised. He saw a compass needle and was puzzled that no matter what he tried, the compass needle always jumped back to its original position. As an old man, when he wrote his autobiographical notes, he tried to recapture this experience with the following words: "That this needle behaved in such a determined way did not at all fit into the nature of events which could find a place in the . . . world of concepts" (p. 9).

What is interesting about this description is, among other things, that when Einstein was an old man and tried to recapture this experience of his childhood, he used animistic language. When he was a child, it seemed to him that the needle "behaved" in a "determined way." This certainly reflects the animistic conception of the world he had as a child and to which reference was made above. His description implies that as a child, on the basis of this experience, he somehow had the notion that the compass needle was guided by a living force or, perhaps, had a will of its own. He then goes on to say that this experience puzzled him because at that time his system of thought was such that the compass needle did not fit.

What was this system of thought? All objects in the world were either animate or inanimate, and the latter, he thought, could move only by direct contact. But the compass needle seemed to fit into neither category. It moved, but not by direct contact, and, yet, it did not seem alive; hence the puzzlement of the child Einstein. The point is this: if Einstein as a little boy had not felt puzzled,

he would not have felt the need to find a better conceptual system. And he had to do it himself.

By explaining too much to children, that is, by providing them with conceptual systems that are not derived from their experiences, we kill their interest. Illa Podendorf's writing avoids this pitfall. In her book she provides children with many experiences that raise questions and challenge childish conceptual systems. She does this brilliantly, especially in regard to natural forces like magnetism, electricity, etc. She never says explicitly whether these forces are animate or inanimate, but one gets the feeling that she is well aware that children today, as in Einstein's days, tend to attribute life to all forces that cause motion. She presents the child with experiences which he must and can interpret himself. She draws the child's attention to the strange behavior of natural objects and forces, and she helps him find as many explanations as he can understand on the basis of these experiences, but she never expects the child to swallow scientific systems far removed from his experience.

In a sense, the experience of the five-year-old Einstein was entirely typical of the experiences of all researchers, young or old. Einstein himself confirms this. According to his own words, he continued to feel a sense of wonder and puzzlement until he was an old man whenever "an experience came into conflict with concepts." It is this sense of wonder and puzzlement that provides the motive for the scientist to search for new solutions and to revise his scientific system. This conflict between facts he experiences and theories he invents motivates him to search for new theories to account for the facts as experienced and for new facts to support or refute his theories. This is of course nothing new. The history of science, at least in modern times, that is, approximately since Galileo, is nothing more than this endless search for new theories to account for ever new facts or experiences.

It would seem that this has very clear-cut implications for the scientific education of children which, strangely enough, are often overlooked. The implication is that the child, just as the adult scientist, must learn to have the courage to look, to observe, to experience. From this it would seem to follow that we must not tell the child one time that his experiences are correct and reliable and another time that they are not. If we do that, we make him distrust his own observations and demand that he trust our words more than his observations. Nothing could be more disastrous for the education of a scientist.

We cannot tell the child when he observes a connection between clouds and rain that he is right but when he observes that the clouds seem to follow him when he walks, that he is wrong. What we can do in the latter case is to encourage him to make additional observations so that he will find his original observations challenged. Similarly, when a child says that he can prove that plants can "feel the light" because they bend toward the light, it may be very unwise to tell him that his observation that plants bend toward the light is correct but that he is wrong in thinking that they can feel the light. By saying that the plants' bending toward the light proves that they can feel it, the child has indicated the level on which he can understand what proof is. To tell him that this is not proof is to tell him that he should revise his thinking regardless of experience. But that is exactly contradictory to what Einstein says: namely, what leads to scientific discoveries is experiences that upset conceptual systems or theories.

In other words, one of my objections to much of modern science education is that the child is introduced to scientific systems, the experiential basis of which he has never grasped. Consequently, such a gap often exists in his mind between experience and scientific system that his experience cannot ever challenge the scientific system. Nor can a scientific system he does not understand challenge him to look for facts and inquire how they are related to the theory. It may be that, if in books and conversations we could provide children with experiences that are puzzling, we would be helping to do a much better job of educating scientists than by insisting that they swallow logical systems that are entirely out of step with their experience.

LITERATURE FOR "CHILDREN WITHOUT"

MARION EDMAN[1]

THE title for this paper calls to mind a statement attributed to John Ciardi, "Fools give short answers to long questions." Certainly either "literature for children" or "children without" requires long answers. It becomes increasingly clear as one tries to find published research and to tap the practical experiences of many people (primarily teachers and librarians) who for long years have tried to bring together the children in culturally deprived areas with the books in their libraries and school rooms. The research is pitifully lacking and the reports of experience almost completely contradictory.

This is a not uncommon frustration in our age when we seem to know the answers, but the questions we do not always know. The discussion of this topic, therefore, might most profitably point the way to questions that must be raised before they can be answered. Only rigorous research, highlighted by carefully evaluated practices in dealing with this special group of children and the ways that will lead them to books and reading, can give us the answers we earnestly seek.

This does not discount the honest efforts many conscientious librarians and teachers have long been engaged in. Perhaps they were the first to discover what the sociologists and the politicians have recently become excited about: the culturally deprived children in our society. It is they who have really understood the importance of bringing these children into the main stream of American life, which the politicians and sociologists now believe necessary if this country is to be transformed into the Great Society.

There are numerous, generally well-known, sociological descriptions or definitions of the culturally deprived. It should be pointed out that cultural deprivation is not monolithic. This phenomenon has many faces and many degrees. While there are no exact figures on what proportion of children and youth might fall into the category of general deprivation, it is estimated to be between one-fifth and one-third of all our children. The proportion is expected to increase. Many, but not all, live in the inner core of our large cities. Despite the disadvantages these children may suffer in varying degree, it should be remembered that a considerable number do achieve success in school, graduate from high school (some even go to college), and find a happy place for themselves in adult life. They may find great pleasure in vicarious experiences far beyond their own circumscribed early beginnings, including their pleasure in the use of libraries and books. Because a child grows up in an area where there is no grass, does not mean, ipso facto, that he has become incapable of imagining a world that has luscious green fields. Sam Levenson, who grew up in Harlem, has promised

[1] I wish to acknowledge the very considerable help I received from Mr. William Curtis, doctoral student at Wayne State University, who interviewed teachers, librarians, and students in the Detroit area and who helped analyze questionnaires and answers from other cities. Thanks are also due the many librarians, teachers, and students who co-operated with us.

to make this point clear in his autobiography *Everything but Money*. Claude Brown, in the story of his childhood in the same city, *Manchild in the Promised Land*, and Betty Smith in *A Tree Grows in Brooklyn* have demonstrated that a degrading sociological and economic environment does not entirely mold the mental and spiritual life of the child. Cultural deprivation may even bring children certain advantages. These children may have seen more of the essential matters of life before they are ten than many more privileged children will see even as adults. Claude Brown speaks of his own experience:

When I was very young—about five years old, maybe younger—I would always be sitting out on the stoop. I remember Mama telling me and Carole to sit on the stoop and not to move away from in front of the door. Even when it was time to go up and Carole would be pulling on me to come upstairs and eat, I never wanted to go, because there was so much out there in that street.

You might see somebody get cut or killed. I could go out in the street for an afternoon, and I would see so much that, when I came in the house, I'd be talking and talking for what seemed like hours. Dad would say, "Boy, why don't you stop that lyin'? You know you didn't see all that. You know you didn't see nobody do that." But I knew I had.[2]

While Claude Brown does not say in his autobiography that he found books an extension or an explanation of the exciting life he was leading, doubtless there are today, in the slums and in the deprived areas in the rural sections of our country, numberless children who are able and eager to accept much of what we have in the way of books and reading to give them. Certainly many of them will look for greater sophistication in books than do usual children of their age. But it is well known that

[2] Claude Brown, *Manchild in the Promised Land* (New York: Macmillan Co., 1965), p. 415.

these children are only a part of the total group, perhaps a small minority, and that it is probably most often this minority who come to the minds of teachers and librarians when they discuss the culturally deprived, for these are the successes in the efforts of these workers. Who among us does not like to think about and talk about his successes?

The culturally deprived for whom books and reading might well be completely out of reach are those who are extremely deficient in their ability to use standard English (the ordinary language of books); those whose reading skills are so extremely limited that they have come to regard print as almost an exquisite instrument of torture; those whose lives have been so warped that they cannot think of themselves as anything but failures, in relation to what they believe society really wants of them; those whose relationships with other persons have been so unsatisfactory that they find it difficult, if not impossible, to identify with real human beings, to say nothing of fictional characters. These are the children with whom this paper is concerned. A brief discussion of their handicaps as they seem to relate to the children's ability to understand and to find empathy with literature follows.

HANDICAPS OF SPEECH

In the area of speech handicaps there is good research. Let me review some of the more significant studies. Two studies by Strickland and Loban have attracted a great deal of attention. The first is a horizontal study, and the second is a longitudinal study of the actual speech patterns of children, using the techniques of modern recording equipment, modern linguistics, and computers. While these studies are not solely concerned with the culturally deprived, they do include children from this segment of society, and thus comparison is possible between them and more favored children.

Strickland found that practically all children in her sample used a wide range of language patterns but that there were differences in their ability to manipulate the variables. Furthermore, ability to use the variables was significantly related to intelligence, mental age, and the occupational status and education of the parents.[3]

Loban's study followed the speech development of some 250 individual cases through thirteen years: kindergarten through twelfth grade. To date two reports of his findings have been published, one for elementary-age children, one for the junior high level.[4] In both reports, Loban established that at all ages studied there was wide variation in children's ability to communicate orally. This was reflected in the amount of speech used, range of vocabulary, complexity of sentence pattern, fluency, correctness of form, and the occurrence of "language tangles" or mazes. Particularly germane to discussion here are his findings relative to underprivileged children. Negro children, especially those newly emigrated from the South, had a number of peculiar difficulties, but particularly with the verb "to be." Loban concludes, "At the kindergarten level on the omission of auxiliary verbs, the low Negro group had five times as much difficulty as the low Caucasian group and sixteen times as much difficulty as the high Caucasian group."[5]

Loban cites numerous other language patterns where the difficulties of Negro children in using standard English are startling and concludes: "Negro children obviously need to listen and to communicate in situations where they can hear more standard usage—not because standard usage is 'correct' but because standard usage helps to provide access to opportunities and entrance to a wider range of social groups."[6] In other words, Negro children, more than any other group, have special need of becoming familiar with the way English is usually spoken and written.

Loban's study is also useful in establishing a positive relationship between proficiency in oral language and all other areas of the language arts: reading, writing, listening. He makes a plea for considering skill in speaking and listening the cornerstone of skill in writing and particularly in reading; in fact, he insists that the school must give children more help in developing facility in oral speech. He makes a special point concerning the culturally deficient child: "The persistently parallel variation of language proficiency and socioeconomic status should not be overlooked. It appears entirely possible that language proficiency may be culturally as well as individually determined. If children reared in families at the least favored socio-economic positions re-

[3] Ruth G. Strickland, "Language of Elementary School Children: Its Relationship to the Language of Reading Textbooks and the Quality of Reading of Selected Children," *Bulletin of the School of Education, Indiana University*, Vol. 38, No. 4 (July, 1962), 131 pp.

[4] Walter D. Loban, *The Language of Elementary School Children* ("Research Report," No. 1 [Champaign, Ill.: National Council of Teachers of English, 1963]), 92 pp., and Loban, *Language Ability: Grades Seven, Eight, and Nine* ("Co-operative Research Project," No. 131 [Washington: U.S. Office of Education, 1963]), 248 pp.

[5] *Ibid.*, p. 236.

[6] *Ibid.*, pp. 237–38.

ceive a restricted language experience, if their early linguistic environment stresses only limited features of language potential, such children may indeed be at a disadvantage in the years at school and in the ones beyond school."[7]

A study of language involving only culturally deprived children of kindergarten age was made by Dominic Thomas under my direction at Wayne State University. Thomas' conclusions were (1) Culturally different children use a smaller number and variety of words to express themselves. They speak in shorter sentences. (2) They use a much larger proportion of incomplete sentences. (3) They use a smaller proportion of mature sentences and elaborate constructions. They tend not to elaborate their ideas. (4) They commit more errors such as verb and subject not in agreement, colloquialisms and slang, omission of auxiliaries, wrong word order, and misuse of prepositions.[8]

Numerous other studies similar in scope to those cited might be cited here, but perhaps these suffice to establish the fact that considerable research indicates that culturally deprived children suffer severe handicaps in their use of language. Does not this research concerning the importance of the child's learning oral communication suggest that libraries, as well as classrooms, become places for talking, as well as reading? Does it not mean that storytelling, reading aloud, dramatization, and discussing books in groups become activities of paramount importance? That all sorts

of audio-visual stimulation for talking precede attempts to motivate reading? Perhaps in children's libraries, at least, all "Quiet, Please" signs must come down.

The research cited does not mean that culturally deprived children cannot communicate effectively in their own society. This they do in a kind of dialect that carries all the meaning they wish or need to convey to their listeners. Linguists insist that for purposes of communication, any system of language which enables the user to convey meaning is a perfectly permissible form of speech. The only trouble with deviation from standard language is that it is not acceptable in all circles and that it often presents barriers to the acceptance of the deviant speaker. Such is the reception given the speech many children bring to school. Worse still, the language that these children are asked to read is not their language and as such cannot establish communication with them. On many counts, it is almost a foreign tongue: there may be differences of vocabulary, of usage, of pronunciation, of stress and rhythm. To the children, however, the books are wrong and they themselves are right, because those individuals who are most important to them use this language.

How to deal with such discrepancies between the language of everyday communication and the language of books is debatable. There are those who insist that, particularly for the young child, we must begin by writing for him in his own tongue. This practice is illustrated in some delightful reading materials prepared for Headstart children in Mississippi. Such sentences as these are accepted as perfectly normal English: "We been swimming down at the pond"; "Me and Jane killed that ole

[7] *Ibid.*, p. 241.

[8] Dominic Thomas, "Oral Language Sentence Structure and Vocabulary of Kindergarten Children Living in Low Socio-Economic Urban Areas" (unpublished Ph.D. dissertation, Wayne State University, 1961).

snake"; "This fish got a mouth like a big smile."[9]

How and when to make the transition from this sort of language to the standard language of literary materials is a subject in need of a great deal of research. The research now available suggests that much work must be done with children's oral speech before change becomes easy. Ruth Golden's efforts in a Detroit high school bear witness to this fact.[10]

It seems important to point out one obstacle in initiating a program of producing and giving the children with deviant language the kind of reading matter that really communicates with them. This is the intransigent position taken by those teachers, librarians, and leaders of minority groups who see the improvement of language as the *sine qua non* of upward mobility and release from slum status. One linguist of note speaks rather bitingly to teachers on this point:

There is one subcultural factor which does affect the language development of these children, and it is one which I wish to touch on now. This factor is the set of attitudes toward language held by the teachers whom Allison Davis would call "aspiring middle class"—as many teachers are. These attitudes are partly learned in the school and college training of English teachers with its monolithic fixation on "correct English" as the main proper outcome of education in English and the language arts. It is a fixation so deep that it is not felt as a subject for question; it overrides whatever work in child development, educational psy-

chology, or methods the teacher may have had, even if these have been more enlightened about language than usual. It is a fixation often nourished in the teacher's own sense that only by parting with his origins, learning correct English, and moving out of the neighborhood has he been able to cut himself off from the foreign, rural, or working-class ways of his parents. And it frequently expresses itself as a demonstration of real love and concern for the children, that they, too, should come up and out and away from a manner of life that is poverty-stricken, universally condemned, and deadended. Negro teachers especially, insisting that they cannot even understand the children whom they understand only too well, bear down brutally on the divergent phonology, "grammar," and usage of Negro children, communicating their own tension to the construction of the child's ultimate trauma about language. In most instances, all the mores of the school sustain them in this unfortunate practice where they should resist it. The alternative to this overemphasis on conformity to "middle class" speech, too, is unfortunate—the idea that the children are so low on the intelligence scale that their case is hopeless, and that the most the school can do is prepare them for the same manual occupations their parents engage in, keeping them off the streets and out of trouble as long as possible.[11]

In summary, then the language disability of the culturally deprived child affects his use of books, perhaps most *particularly* those of literary value. As Artley points out:

Many children are in a position of learning to attach meaning to a printed symbol when the symbol lies outside their spoken vocabulary; to understand a printed ten-word sentence when normally they speak only a disjointed three-word sentence; to interpret a complex sentence when they have difficulty in using simple ones; to follow the organization of a new story they are trying to read when they are unable to tell in logical order the events in

[9] "Pond, Mississippi Action for Community Education" (Edwards, Miss.: Mace Press, n.d. [mimeographed]).

[10] Ruth I. Golden, "Ways to Improve Oral Communication of Culturally Different Youth," in Arno Jewett, Joseph Mersand, and Doris V. Gunderson (eds.), *Improving English Skills of Culturally Different Youth in Large Cities* ("U.S. Office of Education Bulletin," No. 5 [Washington: U.S. Office of Education, 1964]), pp. 100–109.

[11] Donald Lloyd, "Subcultural Patterns Which Affect Language and Reading Ability," in Arno Jewett, Joseph Mersand, and Doris V. Gunderson (eds.), *Improving English Skills of Culturally Different Youth in Large Cities* ("U.S. Office of Education Bulletin," No. 5 [Washington: U.S. Office of Education, 1964]), pp. 117–18.

the familiar "Little Red Riding Hood"; to read complete sentences with expression when they are unable to give emphatic expression to their own ideas; to interpret punctuation marks when they attach no significance to gesture, pantomimes and free play.[12]

Do not these studies of the modern linguists, with their insistence that we respect the language of all children, no matter how "bad," and that we learn to regard their speech as legitimate communication, place upon teachers and librarians the responsibility to demand of authors and publishers the kind of language in books which these children really use? Do the studies not further suggest that we might carefully consider our attitudes toward "proper" language? And, finally, do they not lay upon us the burden of discovering the techniques whereby the gradual transition from "slum" language to "acceptable" norms of speech is accomplished? Does this not all add up to the proposition that we help these children to become, in effect, bilingual?

HANDICAPS OF POOR READING SKILLS

It should be noted that for those children who have not mastered the basic reading skills, books of any sort are to be avoided because all they can do is to give the child a sense of shame and defeat. While the contention of modern reading experts that "Johnny really can read" is true, it is equally true that an appalling number of children are so handicapped in reading ability that they must be classed, at best, as semiliterate. In a recent newspaper release of reading levels for a high school in a depressed area of Detroit, the Board of Education indicated

that in a graduating class of 260 seniors only 50 were reading at grade level on the standardized reading test given at the school.[13] One might well ask what kinds of books the students in such situations might read with guidance and help from teachers, what sorts of books librarians could beguile them into taking for voluntary and recreational reading. Even though the tests given might not be a fair measure of each child's real ability, and certainly not of his potential as a reader, harm has been done in establishing a label for him as an inadequate reader, of which he himself is more or less painfully aware.

While there is a paucity of research that is truly diagnostic in determining the real causes why the culturally disadvantaged child usually has such tremendous problems in learning to read, one fact seems quite clear and that is, as was pointed out earlier, that he has not begun reading with materials that make sense to him, either in language or in subject matter. He has never looked upon reading in terms of my favorite definition for that complex process—a child's definition: "Reading is talk wrote down."

A reading program in any language, at any stage in a student's career, is likely to be effective to the degree that it parallels the language habits that the student has acquired in speaking. In terms of the language usage of all children in relation to reading, many questions concerning needed research have been raised. One writer in the field lists these: (1) What is the process of learning to read, in linguistic and sociological terms? (2) What is dialectology? (3) What is the general dialectical situation in American English? (4) How

[12] A. Sterl Artley, "Oral Language Growth and Reading Ability," *Elementary School Journal,* **53** (February, 1953), 321.

[13] *The Detroit News,* May 1, 1966, p. 1.

does this situation affect the problem of the teacher? (5) How much do we know about regional kinds of dialect differences in American English? How much more can we hope to know? (6) How do these differences as we know them affect the problem of reading in the American dialectical situation?[14]

Has the time now come when the children's librarian, traditionally co-operative with teachers in schools, be provided with an additional staff member: namely, a person trained, not as a librarian, but as an expert who can analyze children's specific reading problems and who can analyze the difficulties that certain types of reading matter give him? In response to a questionnaire the writer sent librarians working with culturally deprived children, over and over the librarians said, "These children need individual help and guidance." However, librarians are not trained as reading specialists. An expert, such as the one proposed, might be able to co-ordinate, more effectively than is now possible, the efforts made by school and library to give children mastery of those basic skills, without which reading of any sort is impossible.

PSYCHOLOGICAL AND SOCIOLOGICAL HANDICAPS

But language is not the only area where the child needs to feel empathy with what he finds in books. Perhaps the psychological and sociological factors involved are far more important than the linguistic ones. The observation has already been made that because of his background the culturally deprived child may be far more sophisticated about some things than are normal chil-

dren of his age. Are the pictures he sees, the characters he meets, the situations presented ones that he can understand and find meaning and delight in? With such questions in mind, several school systems have taken great pains to prepare special materials for the culturally deprived, sometimes with happy, sometimes with disastrous, results.

One program involving the careful preparation of special reading materials for culturally deprived children in Detroit has been described by Gertrude Whipple.[15] Careful consideration was given general content, characters, illustrations, stories, vocabulary, and the teacher's manual. These books thus prepared have now been used with apparent success through the second grade and hopefully will prevent many children from becoming crippled readers even at the earliest levels.[16] To what age levels such contrived material can be used successfully is not yet known.

Much of the work done along these lines, however, has been based on faith rather than on exhaustive research. Does the culturally deprived child gain more from reading that which gives him better understanding of his own world with its real, raw problems of life, exciting and challenging as they are, or should he learn to live vicariously in an entirely strange world of order and respectability, often (to his taste) humdrum and placid? Here the basic question of what our society wants of the culturally deprived becomes para-

[14] Raven I. McDavid, "Dialectology and the Teaching of Reading," *Reading Teacher,* **18** (December, 1964), 206–13.

[15] *City Schools Reading Program* (4 vols.; Chicago: Follett Publishing Co., 1963).

[16] Gertrude Whipple, "The Culturally and Socially Deprived Reader," in H. Alan Robinson (ed.), *The Underachiever: Proceedings of the Annual Conference on Reading Held at the University of Chicago, 1962* ("Supplementary Educational Monographs," No. 92 [Chicago: University of Chicago Press, 1962]), pp. 129–36.

mount: is it greater conformity by making more people middle class in values and habits or is it to play up the strengths of lower-class life, while minimizing its pain and vulgarity? Claude Brown, whose *Manchild in the Promised Land* was mentioned earlier, is one who is still earnestly seeking an answer to this basic question:

Everybody I knew in Harlem seemed to have some kind of dream. I didn't have any dreams, not really. I didn't have any dreams for hitting the number. I didn't have any dreams for getting a big car or a fine wardrobe. I bought expensive clothes because it was a fad. It was the thing to do, just to show that you had money. I wanted to be a part of what was going on, and this was what was going on.

I didn't have any dreams of becoming anything. All I knew for certain was that I had my fears. I suppose just about everybody else knew the same thing. They had their dreams, though, and I guess that's what they had over me. As time went by, I was sorry for the people whose dreams were never realized.[17]

THE HANDICAP OF A POOR SELF-IMAGE

An important factor in their development of values and goals in life is the kind of self-image children form.

In their excellent discussion of ego development among segregated Negro children, Ausubel and Ausubel report the consequences of factors that prevent the growth of normal human relationships and a feeling of inner-self worth for this type of youngster. The segregated Negro child often refuses to identify himself with his own group, because he believes his group is accorded little worth in general society.[18] He bene-

fits little or nothing of derived status from his parents, and so early he associates himself with a peer group, where his activities are often unsuppressed. Here he experiences a freedom that middle-class children rarely have and develops a sure sense of independence; however, he ordinarily feels no great drive for academic success, although he often expresses unrealistically high vocational interests, which may not really be his true or functional level of striving. In general, he misses those "supportive traits [that] include habits of initiative and responsbility, the 'deferred gratification' pattern of hard work, renunciation of immediate pleasures, long-range planning, high frustration tolerance, impulse control, thrift, punctuality and willingness to undergo prolonged vocational preparation."[19]

Sexual differences in these matters are more pronounced for Negro children than for white because the Negro family pattern is more predominantly matriarchal. Bowman reports four negative aspects of the child's self-image in school: a sense of failure, alienation from people, a feeling of always being treated unfairly, and finally, hopelessness concerning the future.[20] Bowman lists five characteristics of a good school program that can help heal the bruised egos that the culturally deprived often bring to the learning tasks set for them, but none of his remedies indicates any part that the right books can play in this healing process.

There are those who feel that school and formal attempts at education of any sort, as presently constituted, do

[17] Brown, *op. cit.*, p. 414.

[18] David Ausubel and Pearl Ausubel, "Ego Development among Segregated Negro Children," in A. Harry Passow (ed.), *Education in Depressed Areas* (New York: Bureau of Publications, Teachers College, Columbia University, 1963), pp. 109–41.

[19] *Ibid.*, p. 118.

[20] Paul H. Bowman, "Improving the Pupil Self-Concept," in Robert D. Strom (ed.), *The Inner City Classroom: Teacher Behaviors* (Columbus, Ohio: Charles E. Merrill Books, 1966), pp. 75–91.

more to increase than to alleviate the feelings of insecurity and inferiority that the culturally deprived child brings with him as he enters into contact with this segment of his world. A recent book describing this process is titled *Education for Alienation*.[21] Many psychologists and sociologists insist that the kindergarten child from the slums is a far healthier individual in his personal and interpersonal relationships than he will be at any later stage of his school life. If this unhappy situation is now true and is to be reversed, what shall be the role of books? Is it by identifying with others in like trouble or is it by identifying with individuals who were successes that these children gain a more favorable perspective of themselves and their rightful place in the society? Should this identification be with their own race or minority group? Should it be with those whose achievements are within the realm of possibility for themselves or with those who were the particularly fortunate unfortunates? Answers to these questions seem now in the realm of the unknown. Here is probably the area where librarians can help most, but perhaps they will need the assistance of trained psychologists.

THE UNIVERSALITY OF CHILDREN'S INTERESTS

All studies of the general interests of culturally deprived children show that they do not vary markedly from those of so-called normal children. They enjoy television and look at the same programs. They laugh at humorous situations; they understand tragic and disappointing ones. They can be led, with appropriate methods, to enjoy rhyme and rhythm, stories of adven-

[21] Nathaniel Hickerson, *Education for Alienation* (Englewood Cliffs, N.J.: Prentice-Hall, Inc., 1966).

ture, stories of animals, stories of real life. In other words, their interests are as broad as life and as wide as the subjects dealt with in books. The key to success here is now, as it has ever been, the interested and resourceful librarian who makes a real study of getting the right book to the right child. A real problem is how to multiply the number of such librarians available to children.

THE PLACE OF LITERATURE

Just exactly what literature should be provided for the culturally deprived child is still a debatable matter among teachers and librarians. For this reason, the following definition of literature for children will be used: that body of children's books which, in the combined judgments of teachers and librarians, has been included in the lists compiled by respected and reputable professional organizations such as the ALA, NCTE, ACEI, and others. These lists include books of a wide variety of formats, dealing with a wide variety of topics and certainly far from equal in that elusive quality, "good literary style." These are the books found on the shelves of the average public library, the books in the school library or the classroom, the books that are being purchased for the special projects now being set up for the culturally deprived. These are the materials now available for use with children.

It is to our advantage, in dealing with culturally deprived children, that we have a broad spectrum of materials from which to choose rather than a narrow range of materials that somehow have been labeled "real" literature. Our clientele presents too broad a spectrum of special problems to be encompassed narrowly. It may well be that research will indicate that we need an even broader range of materials than we now have and that many books must be written with the culturally deprived particularly in mind: special subject matter, special language, special format, special illustrations. These will not be inferior materials, because they will be written by talented authors who are particularly sensitive to the needs of this large segment of our society and who will consciously make use of the extensive research of linguistics, reading experts, sociologists, and psychologists now available. But for here and now we must try to make optimal use of what materials we have: this is the best we can do.

The remainder of this paper describes some ways in which teachers and librarians are introducing literature to culturally deprived children and which practices seem to be bringing results. It is assumed that the work of teachers and librarians, whether public or school librarians, is basically the same, for both groups are seriously concerned with helping children to find meaning and pleasure in books. No attempt will be made to mention specific titles. Many excellent lists are in existence, some of which have been developed for special projects dealing with the culturally deprived.[22]

THE UNIQUE CONTRIBUTION OF LITERATURE

One should, however, point out the importance of one role that literature, in its narrower definition, should play in the reading experience of children. Perhaps its unique function is to present a pattern for the development of those personal and interpersonal values commonly accepted as ideal in our culture.[23] The understanding that such values exist and that they have generally proved satisfying to human beings may be the greatest need of children without. If this be true, there is some evidence that current writers of children's books sidestep the presentation of such values. Chambers found in his study of the output of two major publishing houses for one year that the books he analyzed were typically amoral in the themes with which they dealt.[24] It is likewise true that authorities in the field are often in disagreement concerning the validity of the values that an author attempts to present. Such is the case of *The Empty School House*.[25] Perhaps it is not surprising then that general disagreement exists as to what these children need, what materials will meet their needs, and what the youngsters can and will read. We must have further and continuing dialogue on these matters.

READING INTERESTS AND HABITS OF CHILDREN

It is striking to note that little has been done to identify the specific reading preferences of various groups of

[22] *Gateway English: Development of Reading and English Language Materials for Grades 7–9 in Depressed Urban Areas* (New York: Hunter College of the City University of New York, Curriculum Study Center, October, 1965).

[23] May Hill Arbuthnot, "Developing Life Values through Reading," *Elementary English*, 43 (January, 1966), 10–16.

[24] Dewey Chambers, "An Exploratory Study into the Social Values in Children's Literature" (unpublished Ph.D. dissertation, Wayne State University, 1965).

[25] Compare Shelton L. Root, Jr.'s review (*Elementary English*, 43 [April, 1966], 433–35) of *The Empty School House*, by Natalie S. Carlson (New York: Harper & Row, 1965), with comments on the same book by Arna Bontemps, "Uncle Remus, Farewell," *Bookweek, Fall Children's Issue* (October 31, 1965), p. 3.

children.[26] We have many suggestions from authorities in the field but little or no evidence to support it. Norvell, reporting on the reading preferences of 24,000 students in the fourth, fifth, and sixth grades in New York, found a marked difference in what children preferred and what experts recommended.[27]

If such disparity between what children like and what experts *think* they *should like* is true for "average" children, what credence can be placed in opinions regarding the reading interests and habits of the culturally different? In attempting to answer this question, I submitted a brief questionnaire to librarians who work with culturally deprived children. These were the questions:

1. Is there any evidence that certain formats in books appeal particularly to these children: large print, many pictures, limited size, pages broken with wide margins, short paragraphs, etc?
2. What sorts of language barriers seem to inhibit their reading: vocabulary, many proper names, sentence structure, idioms, dialect of various kinds?
3. Do children of minority groups like to read about traditional figures representing their own group? About "real live heroes" of their group who have succeeded? Do they like pictures of their own race?
4. What kinds of humor appeal to these children? What kinds, if any, appeal particularly to Negro children?
5. Do they seem to prefer idealistic materials such as fairy tales and fantasy or, rather, realistic stories of real children in real-life settings?
6. Do they show any preference for stories laid in the urban living they know best

rather than in settings quite unfamiliar to them?
7. Does television viewing seem to influence reading? Do the adult television programs that many of these children watch, with their emphasis on adult adventure and violence, seem to have much influence?
8. Do these children follow the usual sexual differences of boys and girls in their reading interests, despite the fact that many of them are precocious in their knowledge of sex?
9. Do they show any interest in special literary art forms such as poetry or drama?
10. Can you honestly say slum children are a distinct reading group, or do they represent all the individual differences to be found in any "normal" group of children?

The most striking result obtained from this questionnaire was that there is no general agreement on answers to the questions asked among librarians who work almost solely with the culturally deprived in many different cities of the country; however, a few facts did become apparent as the interviews progressed and the questionnaires were analyzed. One was that all children with limited experience in reading, or those having reading difficulties, tend to choose picture books with large illustrations and a minimum amount of text. If this is typically characteristic of the disadvantaged child, then an emphasis on the picture book is not only important for the early reader but also for children at upper elementary and junior high levels. We must, therefore, reconsider our practice of placing all the picture books in one place for the younger child. Poor readers recognize that such titles are the baby books; thus, the non-reading older child will be found at the magazine rack looking at picture books for adults, rather than choosing what might be more suited to his interest and taste.

Another matter of some agreement is

[26] Jean M. Lepere, "Review of Research in Children's Literature," *A Review of Educational Research*, 31 (1961), 179–87.

[27] George W. Norvell, *What Boys and Girls Like To Read* (Morristown, N.J.: Silver-Burdett Co., 1958), 306 pp.

the interest of minority groups in reading specifically about themselves. Most of the experts, however, insisted that all groups in our society should be represented in books. In essence, these books should realistically portray our society today if the book is concerned with the present. All children like a good, adventurous hero regardless of origin. Illustrations should be true to the situation and mood.

Some librarians identified humor and nonsense books as being specifically of interest to these children, especially Negro children. Others objected and said no such preference could be discerned. All children like a funny story or nonsense book.

Statistics on attendance and circulation figures for children's rooms are not available in Detroit, and the questionnaire to other cities did not include this question, but Countee Cullen library in New York was able to report a sharp rise in library use when the staff was expanded.[28] This is significant because the cry is usually for more books and materials. The implication here is what is needed is a more effective job with what is available. One example cited by Countee Cullen librarians is the stress placed on local community organizations to encourage reading as a habit among disadvantaged youngsters. School visits, reading clubs, guest speakers, and community groups have stimulated a new interest in reading at Countee Cullen; this all demands an expanded staff and a reappraisal of the role of libarian. As was indicated earlier, perhaps in slum areas, librarians *are* more important than books, since it is only through guidance to the right books that many of these children will

dare to attempt any reading at all, to say nothing of developing the habit of turning to books for profit and pleasure. Furthermore, all agencies interested in the slum child need to cooperate in encouraging him to read.

Reaffirmation of this viewpoint came while interviewing ninth, tenth, and eleventh grade boys in the "Upward Bound" program at Cranbrook School near Detroit.[29] These boys, who are certainly characteristic of children without, continually reiterated that they frequented only those libraries where the librarian was a sympathetic guide for their interests. Whether it was homework or reading for pleasure, they identified with the library where encouragement and interest were apparent on the part of a librarian. Some indicated that no place like this was available and therefore they did not use the library.

Good picture books, easy text, high interest, universal heroes, realistic situations: these are the materials that librarians say they need. Expanded, interested staff who make extended community contacts and who are creative and particularly sympathetic with the peculiar problems of children without are needed to get these materials into circulation. In addition to librarians, perhaps other highly trained workers are needed if the library staff is to deal effectively with children without.

TEACHING METHODS AND MATERIALS

Just as the traditional librarian must be remade to fit the new situations, so must the traditional teacher of literature, both in the materials used and in the methods followed, if he wishes to reach this type of child. The old "classics" will hardly do. While being inter-

[28] "Saturday's Children," *Library Journal*, **91** (March, 1966), 1581–90.

[29] Personal interviews with boys at Cranbrook, July 15, 1966.

viewed, the boys at Cranbrook frequently mentioned the titles currently being read in their English classes: *Catcher in the Rye* and *Bridge over the River Kwai.* They were not only reading and discussing these books but were excited by them. Again and again the boys mentioned that *Catcher in the Rye* is about them and their world, that *Bridge over the River Kwai* is an exciting book.

It is important to note that these boys had all been tested and found to be reading far below grade level. Most of them were eleventh graders, but some were as low as fourth grade in reading skills. One was so low that he registered no grade level at all on the test used. It is likewise important to know that in this experiment classes are small and that teachers are well trained and enthusiastic about helping these boys succeed. Much time is spent in oral activities.

While many high schools in many cities have developed special reading materials and suitable methods for presenting these materials, one of special merit has been worked out for the high schools in New York City. In an outline showing how methodology must be suited to characteristics of slow learners, many of the problems of the culturally deprived are covered (although all slow children do not fall into the category of the deprived). Such hints as these are given to teachers: select varied materials that are not too long and that are in line with youngsters' reading skills, interests, and experiences; work on skills needed for understanding; stress experience values in literature rather than literary forms or values; use audio-visual aids, reading by the teacher, class dramatizations, and television to make verbalization con-

crete; stress successes no matter how small; be generous with praise; make assignments short and concrete.[30]

A teacher in the New York City schools has described his success in finding books that made sense to culturally deprived children in terms of their own special concerns. The advice the children seem to be giving their teachers about books was summed up in four points:

1. The subject had to be worth it to us. We like books about animals, aviation, careers, hobbies, sports, the sea, westerns. We love lots of adventure, plenty of excitement, slews of interesting facts about science and things.
2. You couldn't treat us like babies. We may not be so "hot" as readers, but that doesn't mean, if you give us an easy book about ducks on a farm, we'll cackle over it gleefully. We had that stuff in the third grade—remember?
3. You had to give us lots of good pictures, good drawings, and big print. As one of the fellows said, "I can't read when the print on page is so small. After a while I lose my eyesight."
4. You had to know how to write. Maybe the guy who likes to read a lot will stand for some boring parts, but not us! If you want us to read don't beat around the bush; come right to the point. Give us a story that pushes us to go on to the next page and the next page, and you're in![31]

The fact that teachers, as well as librarians, are particularly concerned about these children and are developing special methods for helping them should mean that even closer working relations between school and library will be planned. For these children, more than

---

[30] Joseph Mersand, "Teaching the Slow Learner in English," *High Points,* 49 (May, 1966), 38–53.

[31] Charles Spiegler, "Reading Materials for Retarded Readers," in Helen M. Robinson (ed.), *Materials for Reading: Proceedings of the Annual Conference of Reading Held at the University of Chicago, 1957* ("Supplementary Educational Monographs," No. 86 [Chicago: University of Chicago Press, 1957]), p. 29.

other children, the right hand should know what the left hand is doing to try to help them.

In conclusion, then, what do we make of the fact that we have in our society a considerable number of children whom we designate as children without? What do we wish to give them that books can supply? In a recent editorial discussing the computer age and what it might mean for man, Norman Cousins speaks of the role of the poet, the man of literature, in our total society: "The poet reminds men of their uniqueness. It is not necessary to possess the ultimate definition of this uniqueness. Even to speculate on it is a gain."[32]

One main question now becomes crystal clear. How shall the books we

give him help encourage the child who is without many of the trappings and certainly without some of the values and life patterns we hold dear in our society but who still possesses many ideals that have value for human life? How shall these books help him and us to cherish his uniqueness and special worth in our society?

Claude Brown reminds us that even in the murkiest slums people have their aspirations. He says, "Everybody I knew in Harlem seemed to have some kind of dream."[33] We teachers and librarians can only ask a question in reply: "What books can we find for creating finer dreams and for making these dreams come true for children that fate has given little but dreams to live by?"

[32] Norman Cousins, "The Computer and the Poet," *Saturday Review* (July 23, 1966), p. 42.

[33] Brown, *op. cit.*, p. 414.

SOCIAL VALUES IN CHILDREN'S LITERATURE

SOCIAL values is one of those convenient phrases that has almost no meaning, or perhaps a different meaning for each listener. So, like Alice in Wonderland, I shall have to make a word mean what I want it to mean, in order that we may talk about it together. I define "social values" as the struggles, for good or evil, of people in groups. The more fundamental term would be moral values, under which term we could discuss all the struggles of people to get along with each other, either singly or in groups. To stick, for as long as I can, to social values, I should like to talk about some of the author's problems in writing of things that happen to people in groups. For instance, anti-Semitism is a group disease; if it were an individual disease it would be an entirely different one.

A Canadian librarian wrote me, "I enjoyed reading your book *Berries Goodman*[1] very much, but I was greatly disappointed in Berries' parents. I wish they had been courageous opponents of racism, instead of nice cowards. The mother sold real estate even when she knew about the terrible rules. Thereby she became part of the anti-Semitic system." A part of my reply was, "You are troubled and disappointed that Berries' parents are such nice cowards. This is precisely what I meant them to be and I am delighted that you read it that way." That is, I wanted children to know what anti-Semitism looks like, here in America, in their own communities, to face the possibility that the anti-Semite is not a goose-stepping Nazi seen in a newsreel—the enemy—but might be their own parent, might be their neighbor.

The problem in dealing with the social or moral issue in fiction for children or adults is that the author must not preach, must not make the reader's decision for him, must not indulge in the fallacy that all nice people do good things and that all evil things are done by bad people. The author's job is to throw sharp light on how some real people act in a particular time and place. In this book, if the Goodmans (Berries' parents) had been depicted as heroic contenders against prejudice, every reader would have happily identified himself with them and would have thought, "Oh, yes, that's surely how I would do." And the reader would remain unaware of how easy and nice it might be to be a coward.

Whether children will see this is a strictly justifiable inquiry. They are going to wonder about these parents. It was intended that they wonder. They will not, perhaps as clearly as the librarian mentioned earlier, see that these adults are nice cowards. But I think a child is likely to be left at least with a question, a puzzlement about the grownups in this book. Why are they like this? Is this the way people are? And this may make a child look a little more closely, a little more acutely at the people around him.

There is another approach to the author's problem within our definition

[1] Emily Neville, *Berries Goodman* (New York: Harper & Row, 1965).

of social values. Let me quote: "He went up from there to Bethel; and while he was going up on the way, some small boys came out of the city and jeered at him, saying 'Go up, you baldhead! Go up, you baldhead!' And he turned around, and when he saw them, he cursed them in the name of the Lord. And two she-bears came out of the woods and tore forty-two of the boys."[2] Thus speaks Elijah in the books of Kings in the Bible. Like most good books, this one can be read by children and adults at different levels. This is, in a way, practically a classic plot of a children's book. Here were the bad boys, they were disrespectful, and they were punished—twenty-one boys to a bear.

In a sense something of the same treatment might have been devised for the people who were anti-Semitic in my book; I could have arranged a bear to dispose of them. I could have made them more wicked, so that it would have been perfectly evident that they should be punished. But the story in the Bible starts from complete certainty, a kind of certainty that few of us have. If one is writing from the basis that fear and love of the Lord are the guiding principles, it is quite clear that anybody who is disrespectful to the Lord should be punished and if necessary by a she-bear. But the author today is living in this world in which there is a good deal of confusion, and it is difficult to take an absolute stand, to be totally against one group of people. In one of the many conferences I had with my editor, Ursula Nordstrom, while re-writing "Berries," she said worriedly, "But,

Emily, you *are* against anti-Semitism aren't you?"

"Uh, well—yes," I said, but I was worried, too. As an author, I was trying to muster all my abilities to *show* anti-Semitism, and to show it I have virtually to feel it. I have to feel that I, too, could be like Berries' mother or even Sandra's mother. I cannot decide I am totally against them before I begin writing. I cannot have my she-bear ready in the wings.

The problem is that for an author to feel as a group is difficult. In writing about people, the author is writing about single people, individuals. I can write about what single people do in groups, but I must keep my focus on the individual. In books of some years back, for example *Lorna Doone,*[3] which is a good rousing story, there is hidden behind the action a very neat sort of satire on the stupidity of the people who surrender to the bandits because the bandits seem heroic. Louisa May Alcott also attacks the false fronts and manners of people behaving conventionally and making a great show of politeness when they are actually backbiting.[4] In Louisa May Alcott's books there is a variety of very short personal descriptions of people and very accurate conversations and detailed descriptions of people, mixed sometimes with very sentimental moralizing which children of nine or ten never hear. This aspect of children's reading should be kept in mind when we worry about books solving problems rightly or wrongly. Most of the time the child is not listening; he is waiting to see what happened. In the other older books,

[2] II Kings 2:23–24, Revised Standard Version (New York: Thomas Nelson & Sons, 1959).

[3] Richard D. Blackmore, *Lorna Doone.*

[4] Louisa May Alcott, *Jack and Jill.*

those that I grew up with, there was not much attempt at any social issue. There was individual heroism, whether the hero was a dog loyal to his master as in *Greyfriars Bobby*[5] or whether it was a knight in armor, as in *The Black Arrow*.[6] There are modern equivalents, such as *Arm of the Starfish*[7] and *Shadow of a Bull*,[8] in which personal heroism is really the theme.

There are, in recent literature, a good many books in which authors are trying to deal with social values—with integration, with anti-Semitism—and have spoken well because they have kept their focus on the individual. When an author tackles an issue like integration or segregation or anti-Semitism by inventing some puppets to fight the battle for him, he is wasting time. If his main object is to present his own point of view he should sit down and write an essay or a few paragraphs to tell people what he believes. He does not need to create puppets and dragons to be slain. The following are some books in which the authors write with conviction and effectiveness about important issues.

In Natalie Savage Carlson's *The Empty School House* she writes about a little Negro girl, Lullah, and her white friend, Oralee. The two have had a quarrel, but Lullah takes Oralee a birthday present to make up.

"Happy birthday," Lullah said to her.
I think Oralee would have made up with Lulluh then and there and asked her stay for the rest of the party.

[5] Eleanor Atkinson, *Greyfriars Bobby* (New York: Harper & Bros., 1912).

[6] Robert Louis Stevenson, *The Black Arrow*.

[7] Madeline L'Engle, *Arm of the Starfish* (New York: Ariel Farrar, Straus & Cudahy, 1966).

[8] Maia Wojciechowska, *Shadow of a Bull* (New York: Atheneum Publishers, 1964).

But Lily [the older sister] yelled at Lullah, "You've got no business here. You weren't invited."
"Yeah!" Myrtle said. "Who invited you?"
I saw Lullah look pleadingly at Oralee. But Oralee just stood there and hung her head . . . stood there looking ashamed and saying nothing.[9]

It is likely that any child reading this would see how probable it is that she herself would do the same thing. It is very hard for a child to stand up for one friend when there are two or three friends on the other side saying, "we don't want her," whether the one child is a Negro or white child or just some child who is for some reason not "in" with the crowd. Thus an author speaks of a social issue in terms that children would recognize and understand.

In the book *Roosevelt Grady* by Louisa Shotwell there is nothing in the text to say specifically that the boy is a Negro or that the author is seeking to evoke the reader's interest in the social condition of a minority group. But the reader is very strongly involved with the individuals and the family. The mother takes the children to a doctor, and he has given them a rather complicated ritual for giving pills at three-hour intervals, washing the silver separately, and so on. One of the boys, Matthew, also has a congenitally bad foot.

He held up his bad foot and Dr. Bates felt of it, all around.
"Why didn't you have something done about this foot three years ago?" he said to Mamma, rather cross-like . . .
"Doctor Bates," she said, "I think I'd best tell you something. We follow the crops for a living. Right now we're living in one room, all six of us. We got no clock to measure taking medicine by. We got no ice box. What we eat with, it isn't silver, it's tin, but we keep it clean . . .

[9] Natalie Savage Carlson, *The Empty School House* (New York: Harper & Row, 1965), p. 89.

"About Matthew's foot, his papa and I, we never knew it might be fixed. Even if we had the money to pay to leave him in the hospital, the Lord alone knows where we'll be in three months time, and He may be in some doubt Himself. Folks got to do what they can with what they got and that's what we do. We make out. And thank you kindly, Doctor Bates. How much do I owe you for these pills?"

When Mamma stopped talking, Doctor Bates looked . . . like a little boy the teacher had scolded.[10]

A child reader would see Dr. Bates's failing: as an individual, he was too "stuck up" about his doctoring.

Mary Stolz in *The Noonday Friends* shows Franny and her noonday friend, whom she has time to talk with only at lunch because they are busy at home with their housework and helping their mothers. Franny's father seems to be unable to hold a job most of the time which is the reason for trouble in their house. Mary Stolz shows Franny's father floundering through an answer to a question that Franny asks him.

That evening Franny said to her father, "Is it harder to get a job in America if you're a foreigner?" . . .

He sighed a bit, put his newspaper down, and said, "Yes. I'm afraid under most circumstances it is."

"Why?"

"Oh, Franny. Oh, Franny." He stared around the room "I can't give you an answer, just like that. It's how things are."

"But it isn't fair, is it?"

"No."

"Then why did it turn out that way?"

". . . you find as you get older that life does not usually undertake to be fair or logical. Please don't ask me to explain that."[11]

Franny's father is hardly heroic; he has not solved the problem or even in-

dicated where a solution might be. But it gives the child reader something to think about. Is there a solution? Where is it?

And, finally, one of the best examples is not from recent literature but from a well-known author-friend, Mark Twain. Many of you remember the passage in which Huck is wondering whether to help return Jim to his owner. Mark Twain really pulls the reader's leg and tweaks his nose through two pages of considering how wicked Huck would be if he befriended Jim and how good he would feel if he turned him in. At one point Huck says he just can't help the way he is because "I was brung up wicked." But then he decides that he will try writing a note to turn Jim in and see if he doesn't feel better when he has done this. "I felt good and all washed clear of sin for the first time I have ever felt so in my life, and I knowed I could pray now. But I didn't do it straight off, but laid the paper down and set there thinking—thinking how good it was all this happened so, and how nearly I came to being lost and going to hell." Then he thinks over his life with Jim.

But somehow I couldn't seem to strike no places to harden me against him, but only the other kind. I'd see him standing my watch on top of his'n, 'stead of calling me, so I could go on sleeping . . . I struck the time I saved him by telling the men we had smallpox aboard, and he was so grateful, and said I was the best friend old Jim ever had in the whole world, and the *only* one he's got now; and then I happened to look around and see that paper [the note he had written to tell the lady she could get back her runaway slave].

It was a close place. I took it up, and held it in my hand. I was a trembling, because I'd got to decide, forever, betwixt two things, and

---

[10] Louisa Shotwell, *Roosevelt Grady* (Cleveland, Ohio: World Publishing Company, 1963), pp. 71–80.

[11] Mary Stolz, *The Noonday Friends* (New York: Harper & Row, 1965), pp. 79–81.

I knowed it. I studied a minute, sort of holding my breath, and then says to myself: "All right, then, I'll *go* to hell!" and tore it up.[12]

It is interesting that, despite the satire and the fact that in a way the reader always knows how Huck is going to decide, there is considerable feeling of the tension of a person making a decision. This is very realistic, and anyone who has had to make a decision recognizes the feeling.

Twain stirred up a good deal of consternation in his day by his jabs at Christianity. Actually he was equating pious Christianity with pious fraud. His book was banned from the children's room of a Brooklyn library, and apparently a librarian wrote an angry letter to him which he answered by saying, "I wish I could say a softening word or two in defense of Huck's character since you wish it. But really, in my opinion his character is no better than that of Solomon, David and the rest of the sacred brotherhood." Here Twain is being very satiric, of course, poking his finger at the pious Christian's tendency to ignore the rather large size failings of David and Solomon. But at the same time, right in the same words, I think he quite honestly meant to compare Huck with David, because I am sure Twain considered David (not just David and Goliath, but the whole David) one of the truly heroic figuers in all literature.

Against the background of this discussion I can state that social issues are to me unimportant. It is how individuals act that is of major concern. Some of the time as an author I am interested in how they act in groups, but a great deal of the time I am interested in how

they act individually. Perhaps most often I am interested in how children act with their parents. It seems to me that the way a child learns to love and hate in his own family must have a great deal to do with how he acts when he confronts situations of anti-Semitism, integration, and similar critical social issues. The way he learns how to handle love and hate at home is probably going to affect him most of his life.

A good many people have written me about the matter of whether Dave, the boy in *It's Like This, Cat*,[13] respects his father, and they asked why I didn't give him a father who commanded respect. This is very similar to the problem with Berries Goodman's parents. But parents in this world are not perfect. The job of an author is to reassure children that other adults know this, that they can write about a parent who is imperfect. The job of the author is not to solve the child's problem: that is, he doesn't have to show his child hero a satisfactory way to cope with a prejudiced, a drunken, or a lazy parent.

This is perhaps one of the great differences in the novels of today compared with those of the Victorian era. It is not so much that we have progressed to social issues or moral issues or more mature issues. The difference is in how neatly we solve the problems. Many of the books written in earlier decades dealt with some of the same problems, but there was a tendency in adult literature as well as in children's to have every problem neatly disposed of. In a book called *The End of American Innocence*[14] the author, Henry

[12] Samuel Clemens, *The Adventures of Huckleberry Finn* (New York: Harper & Bros., 1923), pp. 228–29.

[13] Emily Neville, *It's Like This, Cat* (New York: Harper & Row, 1963).

[14] Henry F. May, *The End of American Innocence; A Study of the First Years of Our Own Time, 1912–1917* (New York: Alfred A. Knopf, Inc., 1959).

May, advances the theory that, until American idealism had been safely buried in Flanders' Fields, a belief in the happy ending was as imperative in philosophy as it was essential in fiction. This attitude seems to have carried over to children's fiction. It was in this era that people rewrote the "Three Little Pigs" so that no little pig need die.

In an earlier paper in this conference Mrs. Luitgard Wundheiler spoke about the children's realistic and often erroneous interpretation of natural events: "when I move, the cloud moves." A reasonable and logical explanation to that child that this is not true is not likely to be meaningful and is likely to frustrate the child because it is in terms he does not understand. There is quite a parallel in creative fiction, and the implications suggest that one should not make judgments for the child. What fiction does is to show him the raw materials: the clouds and the trees are the scientific raw material; people loving and hating and going about their business are fictional raw material. A good example is *The Rock and the Willow*[15] by Mildred Lee. This is a book that ends with a number of questions. The heroine's father gets to the bus too late, they would like to have told each other how much they loved each other, and at the last minute they both failed again.

The need for a hero and a conclusion is mainly artistic. It makes a more satisfying book. People generally like to feel entertained when they are reading, and it is nice to have all problems solved at the end.

Finally, in this discussion of values and morals in children's literature, we should be reminded to look closely at the *way* an author expresses himself, at his style of writing. Style is no added frill. The choice of word and phrase fixes the author's values. There is what I call the "Twinkling Blue Eyes school of description." A twinkling blue-eyed lad is obviously the hero as surely as someone else who is the "son of the richest man in the county" is hopeless, hung for a villain already. Here, from Henry Felsen's *Crash Club*, are a few lines of what I consider good description. The author writes about teen-agers and hot rods and fads, and he writes honestly with no false heroes. In introducing the leading girl in *Crash Club* he says, "Like her movie favorites, she kept her mouth open a good deal, her tongue lightly caught between her even, white teeth. The way she acted called attention to herself as a girl, rather than as a person."[16] You know quite a lot about that girl in two sentences. Perhaps as much as you'll ever want to know.

Another example is one of many in Frank Bonham's *Durango Street*. Speaking of a juvenile delinquent who has been in prison and is home on parole to his mother, the author writes: "He had had to learn to get along without her affection, the way fat people get along without sweets."[17] The reader knows what the trouble is between the boy and his mother, that she is not giving him any affection, but he still has not learned to get along without it.

The descriptions of the hero and heroine in realistic fiction should be as precise as these examples. The idea is not necessarily to create a hero with whom the reader will want to identify

[15] Mildred Lee, *The Rock and the Willow* (New York: Lothrop, Lee & Shepard Co., 1963).

[16] Henry G. Felsen, *Crash Club* (New York: Random House, 1958), p. 28.

[17] Frank Bonham, *Durango Street* (New York: E. P. Dutton & Co., 1965), p. 23.

himself constantly. This is a problem to the author because in a sense the reader is supposed to identify himself with the hero. It is possible, but not simple, to create a hero whose career the child will want to follow while avoiding the trappings of a false hero. In an English book titled *Into the Forest* by Rosamund Essex there is a line that expresses what I think about the writing. There are three children; one is blind, one deaf, and one crippled. She speaks of Hadrian, the deaf boy: "Living as he did in a silent world, he liked to think and dream and make up wonderful stories in which he was always the hero."[18] This may be what too many books have encouraged children to do. This is not a bad experience in itself, but it can go too far. If I have any mission as an author, it is to show the reader, not how great a hero he could become, because I don't think most people are going to become heroes, but simply how hard it is to be a plain decent human being. The writer, and the reader, of children's books does indeed need a sense of values, whether the background of the story is social or mainly personal. The values that I write about will not lead to greater heroics; only, I hope, to fuller humanity.

[18] Rosamund Essex, *Into the Forest* (New York: Coward-McCann, Inc., 1965), p. 18.

POETRY FOR CHILDREN

DAVID MC CORD

WHEN I was twelve, my family headed West to live on my uncle's homestead ranch in the south of Oregon. We lived there three years in all: no light, heat, power; no, not even water, except what we could pump by hand. I milked the cow, raised chickens, did the chores, but had no schooling through the critical years of twelve to fifteen. For one year, once a week, I did take the train to Grants Pass, down the great Rogue River, and was tutored by a fine, wise German lady who spoke four languages and wrote poetry. In the main, though, I was on my own to learn the language of the wild, and learn it on a real frontier; for Jackson County, Oregon, was still a wilderness when I was a boy, and I am very grateful for that rare experience. It taught me more, I think, than anything else about the essential poetry of life. It taught me, in a profusion of wildflowers, in a time of drought, in the terror of a forest fire, to honor the earth itself.

In any discussion about children's verse, writing children's verse, and the audience for children's verse so far as I have dealt with it, I must confess that I really know nothing about the audience —or at least no more about it than any person past a certain age knows about the arcane world of children. Once in a while we glimpse that world—but ever so briefly—as it was when we were young. Some years ago while returning from the funeral of an old friend, Frederick Winsor, author of *A Space Child's Mother Goose*, I put together what is possibly the only American limerick written as a deeply serious poem. It became the Invocation to *Take Sky*.

> Blesséd Lord, what it is to be young:
> To be of, to be for, be among—
> Be enchanted, enthralled,
> Be the caller, the called,
> The singer, the song, and the sung.[1]

That is perhaps what youth is and always was. But in saying so we haven't gone very far from Stevenson's "Looking Forward":

> When I am grown to man's estate
> I shall be very proud and great,
> And tell the other girls and boys
> Not to meddle with my toys.

For children haven't changed—have they?—basically much from that.

And just because I believe they haven't, I would like to offer a few of the rules that guide my writing. Although they may not seem to amount to anything, unconsciously they have exercised control whenever I have attempted verse for children. First, just be a child before you grow up and let nothing interfere with the process. Write it all *out* of yourself and *for* yourself as you remember that weasel body with the eagle eyes. Next, never take the phrase "writing verse *for* children" seriously. If you write *for* them you are lost. Ask your brain's computer what you know about a child's mind and what goes on inside it. The answer is zero. What do they think of this new world

---

[1] From *Take Sky*, copyright © 1961, 1962, by David McCord, with permission of Little, Brown and Company.

53

which you don't even pretend to understand? They do not compare it with the past. It is the only world they know. Don't ever think you are looking at the young; just make sure the young are looking at you. Make your readers believe you are letting them into your own dark life, into your own serene confusion, not you into theirs. Children move forward on a kind of belt line. And when I say they are all the same basically when very young, I am well aware that they change from grade three upward under the flux and impositions and controls of our time—if we have controls. Well, they do move on a sort of belt line, moving steadily through eight grades up through high school, on through college. But the province I am considering is bounded by grades two or three and eight. Now when the young climb on this belt line they are all, or surely 70 to 80 per cent of them, potential poets; but when they leave this belt line—and some of them are thrown off just before they reach the end—I may suppose that only .15 or .25 of them are poets. Something is killed in them. It isn't strange that it is killed in our time, even less strange that it was killed in my time. I don't know whose fault this is. Of course it is partly the fault of time; for did not Thomas W. Lamont once say in substance: The only thing wrong with youth is that it doesn't last? Phyllis McGinley says:

> Darkness delays. The skipping rope
> Twirls in the driveway after dinner.[2]

What wonderful lines these are! They condense so much about one last and almost perfect fragment of lost youth. For those who agree that being a little

girl does end at age thirteen, I recommend Miss McGinley's flawless poem called "Portrait of Girl with Comic Book."[3] No other poem to my knowledge offers such incredible insight into a child's mind at the happiest and saddest turning point of life.

I now have to say that I am afraid of children. I suppose they have always frightened me since I knew so much of solitude at one phase of my life. But I have learned somewhat to overcome that fear. I have spoken a good deal at book fairs in Chicago, Cleveland, Detroit, Flint, Boston, Providence, and elsewhere to quantities of children, though I haven't yet got over the sorry truth that this is the only audience in the world that chills me. Most audiences I thoroughly enjoy. But if children remain a somewhat frightening group, they are also a bland, gay audience as far as the writer goes, because he does not normally see the child's reaction to the poem or book. Of course he gets letters from children, and they are almost always encouraging. Some marvelous letters from children have come my way. I have said that you don't know what goes on in the minds of children. And you don't, as you write, really know what their reaction is going to be except for this steady trickle of letters.

On reflection, it is comforting to realize that children still do skip and slide and jump and skate and fish and swim and walk and ride and row and paddle and camp out and splash in puddles and swell with poison ivy. They play with tops, and they love horses, donkeys, cows, pigs, dogs, and cats. They catch bugs and frogs and turtles, newts and garter snakes and butterflies, and yet know less—far less—about rough farm

<hr/>

[2] Phyllis McGinley, "June in the Suburbs," *The Love Letters of Phyllis McGinley* (New York: Viking Press, 1954), p. 103.

[3] *Ibid.*, p. 11.

life than we did. But, curiously enough, a lot of them know more about birds than we ever managed because of feeding stations, bird talks on television, recorded birdsong, and other things. Some of these children—in spite of all statistics—*really* read, all of them can listen, and a few of them will.

Well, where does children's verse begin? Of course it begins with nursery rhymes, with the counting out rhymes, with

"Fire, fire," said Mrs. McGuire.
"Where, where?" said Mrs. Ware.
"Downtown," said Mrs. Brown.
"Oh, Lord save us!" said Mrs. Davis . . .

or with "Mary Had a Little Lamb," for I suppose that "Mary" is still said by children. I do know that "Mary Had a Little Lamb" is considered by Iona and Peter Opie (with supporting evidence) in *The Oxford Dictionary of Nursery Rhymes*[4] to be perhaps the best known verse in the English language. Is it odd that this is so? Not at all. What is the most beautiful line in the English language? A silly question. No one can say. Or what is the most famous line? Who can guess? The candidates are many: "For old, unhappy, far-off things, / And battles long ago," "My mind lets go a thousand things, / Like dates of wars and deaths of kings," or "Magic casements, opening on the foam / Of perilous seas, in faery lands forlorn." According to G. K. Chesterton the most beautiful line, the most *poetic* line, is only six brief words—"Over the hills and far away." This thesis is supported by such noted poets as Gay, Swift, Burns, Tennyson, Stevenson, and Hen-

ley—all of whom have taken that line as their very own. I mean: they put no quotes around it.

I come now to another look at children, from a different vantage point, in a book called *Children Are Poets* by Susan Nichols Pulsifer.[5] Mrs. Pulsifer works with children who are writing verse, and she has set down some of their poems just as they have written them; and at the end of her book a number of these poems are in the child's own hand. All this reveals succinctly what I have long suspected, that the child not only is a potential poet but every now and then is likely to write a line that any older person would be glad to have written. For example, in *Children Are Poets* one child says,

Now hold this big shell to your ear—
And you will hear
The great big Ocean roar

If there is nothing remarkable about that, let us see what the boy (for he is a boy) says next:

Do little shells
Sing little seas
We never heard before?

Quite remarkable. Any child's poet would be delighted to sign his name to that. Or this by a little girl who is learning something:

I'm learning to ride,
I'm learning to trot,
I'd like to gallop away—why not?

I remember very well—indeed, I shall never forget—a little boy eight years old who won first prize in an essay contest. I was serving on a committee to judge some essays written by young-

[4] Iona and Peter Opie, *The Oxford Dictionary of Nursery Rhymes* (Oxford: Clarendon Press, 1951); *The Oxford Nursery Rhyme Book* (New York: Oxford University Press, 1955).

[5] Susan Nichols Pulsifer, *Children Are Poets* (Cambridge, Mass.: Dresser, Chapman & Grimes, Inc., 1963). Poems used with publisher's permission.

sters in a boy's club over in Charlestown near Boston, a somewhat underprivileged part of the city, so far as the young are concerned. The subject of the essays to be written was *Kindness,* and a lot of small participants wrote warmly about being kind to animals, birds, and so on. But this little boy wrote an essay worth remembering. It won the first prize, hands down. I met him and talked with him, and we put the essay on the radio. It did not seem possible that a child could have written it; and yet, on the other hand, it did not seem possible that a grownup could have written it, either. In some ways much less possible. I talked with the librarian, a marvelous woman who works with these underprivileged boys. She knew this young author and was sure that no one had helped him in any way. On the subject of kindness, here is what the contestant wrote:

> How was the little boy to understand? He had never found a hat before. He had never really found anything which belonged to anybody else. To be sure, he had picked up bright pebbles, dead beetles, and even lighted fire-flies, but nobody had claimed any of these things. In fact, nobody seemed to want them, even for gifts. The little boy felt very happy with the hat on his head. Now he could be a soldier. He could be a cowboy. He could be a bandit and pretend that he was a grown man. And he could be kind and give it away.

Well, we come to other matters about writing verse for children. What does one write about? As I have said, you write out of your own childhood *for yourself.* This is the first principle. Never objectively say there is a little girl, a little boy somewhere. I shall write something that I know will amuse them. I think I saw something that they

did or were doing today or something that I overheard—this is what they would like to hear. You will never be a child's poet following that procedure. You will never be a child's poet anyway. Writing verse for children should be strictly a happening in a poet's life. Forget that we live in a baffling world. That isn't the way to approach it. There is a much simpler way. What you have to remember is that Emerson once said, "Every word was once a poem."[6] Don't forget that. Every word except the articles and a few prepositions. Every word *was* once a poem: there is no room for argument. Take *sky, wind, sea, land, valley, mountain, river, cloud, tree, bird.* All these are very simple words. They *must,* each one of them, have been a poem to the man or woman who invented or first said them. One thinks of *sea,* for example: *sea*—with that long *ē* sound of it opening up the way the sea does on the horizon. *La mer* doesn't open up that way to me; but then I am not French, so I can't tell what it does to a Frenchman. *Thalassa* (Greek) to me is the sound of lapping waves. German *See?* Well the look of that is nearer *sea* than *mer* or *thalassa,* but only *sea* in the Anglo-Saxon sense does open up. On the other hand, *plain* (with the long *ā* of the German *See* in it) also opens up. *Hill* seems to me the right word for hill and nothing else would satisfy. *Brook* for brook. But if you take the French *ruisseau,* well, that too has a wriggly sound to it, like the wandering stream which it is. Of almost equal importance in my credo is something else said by Emerson: "The sky is the daily

[6] Ralph Waldo Emerson, "The Poet," *Essays: Second Series* (Boston: Phillips, Sampson & Co., 1854), p. 23.

bread of the eyes."[7] For so it is. One of my high school teachers in Portland, Oregon, said to us once in class: "Never let a day go by without looking on three beautiful things." How could one ever forget such an aphorism? I have used it in commencement addresses in schools, I have used it in colleges, and have been surprised by the underground return-drift of reaction to find that the young had respect for it. The sky, of course, is one of the first three things you look at —a constant, a natural.

Children today are out of touch with the elements. They fly through one, ski and surfboard in another, hot rod over a third. This is one of the great difficulties a poet has to face. The jet has shrunk this world to the size of an orange, and people soar over great tracts of wilderness that they never, in my day, would have dreamed of seeing. But they are not *in* it. They fly into camp equipped with an outboard motor and all the rest of civilization's mess. They don't go in by canoe and portage. I grew up on a noble salmon and steelhead river and I have since fished a great deal in Canada. I once tutored a boy to enter Andover, and we were rewarded by a 120-mile canoe trip in Canada with one French-Indian guide. Among other things, we caught a baby loon. That in itself was a large experience—the working draft of a poem. Today we would be flown in and flown out. One might as well go camping in a city park. I said to someone a while ago that one of the tragedies of our time is that a boy will have flown to the height of thirty thousand feet before he ever climbs a mountain. All the wonder of going up on his own two feet will come long after he first took wing. Why bother?

I once met a teacher—a born teacher —who knew that her children all came by car to school. It was a rural school; and in coming and going by car they avoided the chance of getting wet. So one day the teacher took them all out in the rain and got them good and soaked. She made them turn their faces up and get the rain all over their faces and let it drip off their noses. Then they came in and she asked them their reactions. What did they think about this and that? What they thought was recorded on the blackboard line by line, and in the end the children had a poem. Those lucky youngsters suddenly had something beyond the comic book, television, a movie, and boredom. The moral is that one ought to make sure that children do know something about the elemental world outside. For example— how does today's youngster read a nature book? I read, when I was a small boy, eight or ten of the volumes of Charles G. D. Roberts: *Red Fox, Kindred of the Wild, The Watchers of the Trails, The Feet of the Furtive,*[8] and so on. Sir Charles was a Canadian, one of their first fine writers about nature. *Tarka the Otter* by Henry Williamson[9] is the greatest animal story, I am positive, since Roberts' *Red Fox*. But I doubt that children are exposed to books like this today. They get diluted reports on natural history; though of

[7] *Emerson's Journals,* ed. Ralph Waldo Emerson and Waldo Emerson Forbes (Boston: Houghton Mifflin Co., 1911), **6,** 410 (May 25, 1843).

[8] Charles G. D. Roberts, *Red Fox* (Boston: L. C. Page, 1905) ; *Kindred of the Wild* (Boston: L. C. Page, 1904) ; *The Watchers of the Trails* (Boston: L. C. Page, 1904) ; and *The Feet of the Furtive* (New York: Macmillan Co., 1913).

[9] New York: Random House, 1960.

course every now and then a best seller will come along, like Sterling North's *Rascal*,[10] an unpretentious, deeply human book about a raccoon. But the truth is that children are not in touch with nature. I have talked with too many of them not to know this for a fact.

A year ago I went down to a grade school in Rhode Island several times—teaching fifth graders poetry—just to get the feel of the audience. One day I asked them about gulls. There were gulls all around them, for the school was close to the water. Did they know what a "thermal" is and why gulls spiral up over a thermal without flapping their wings—especially toward evening? No, they had never watched that performance. I don't know why they hadn't. It was going on right at their doorstep. Now gulls go up on thermals—for example, over smokestacks—soar way up until they are specks, and then level out to descend on long inclines seven or eight miles, perhaps, to their island for the night. They don't have to work to get home. Another thing, I reminded them: the starlings fly in and out of our great cities at dawn and dusk. In Boston they fly right down Commonwealth Avenue in front of my apartment, and I have estimated their flight at probably two million a day. At dawn they go out just as straight as if they flew on a beam at an airport—out to the city dumps or wherever they do their often-destructive work, and they come back at night to sleep on electric signs in winter, for it is very cold at times in Boston, and that warms them up. It is quite an awesome sight to watch these little birds sailing through the coldest gusty weather. Why don't their wingpits freeze?

[10] New York: E. P. Dutton & Co., 1963.

Another thing I would tell them: I used to catch red newts when I was small. Newts, of course, are not easy to find except immediately after rain. But frogs are always available; I don't mean available for one to hurt them but available to any child to study. But do they study them? Do they know the queer things frogs will do? Often, when I am fishing, a frog will be sitting on a big rock, and I'll put a fly out—not to hook him, just to catch his attention. During several casts he will look straight ahead; but finally, like an old man shifting in his chair, he will turn clumsily round and look at the fly with evident delight. And then I put it on the other side and after a long time he comes way around through 180° and he looks at it again. Well, you can roll off your log laughing at such a frog.

Down on the Cape one day when I was trout fishing in a cranberry bog I passed a big frog, and he jumped out of the way. But when I came back, he didn't. So I tickled him with the end of my rod until he would snap at it. Or I would put it under his leg and he would lift his leg but not enough to jump. Then suddenly I had the bright idea of picking a handful of hard, red cranberries—hard, indeed, as marbles. I shot one out in front of my frog the way one shoots a marble, and he grabbed it. So I shot another, and he took it in. And so on, until he had six in his mouth. His mouth was then full to baggy, and he began to drool. These were hard cranberries, and he is not a cranberry eater anyway. Finally, of course, all the cranberries became as slippery as a watermelon seed. One shot out of his mouth; but as soon as it shot out he jumped a few inches and took it in again. For five minutes he sat there unloading cranberries and taking them all back in. A child would have folded up with laughter.

Now the accidents of humor are nearly always brief. Brief, too, are the kinds of poems that children care for. So I talked to the Rhode Island fifth graders on the advantage of brevity. A surgeon friend of mine once received a letter from a very witty friend of his. This witty friend and some more of us were all at a house party. Call the witty friend Mr. X. Mr. X wrote his bread and butter letter: "Dear Bob: Some parties deserve a letter. Some don't. Yours does. Here's mine." You can't cut a word out of that, you see. A fine example of a letter to give to the young.

The other tragedy about ourselves and youth today is that we have lost the art of reading aloud. Children in general (I lack statistics) are not read aloud to unless by teachers and librarians. Especially the librarians. My grandmother read me the Bible through —the King James Version, all the magnificent parts of it—twice before I was twelve. That had a great deal to do with conditioning my instinctive feeling for rhythm and my passionate love of words and the right order of words, and whether adjectives are availing or not —not available, but availing. "Up the airy mountain, / Down the rushy glen," and there you have two adjectives. You are telling children to throw out adjectives, which is sound advice. But suppose you take out *airy* and *rushy*. What is left? "Up the mountain, / Down the glen." But the glory of that fragment is, "Up the *airy* mountain, / Down the *rushy* glen." Children can see that, if a person reads the words slowly aloud.

Once I was talking (in verse) about my Pennsylvania ancestors who were farmers, some of them, and I was say-

ing, "But what old other joys outweigh the land?" Now if I had written, "But what other old joys outweigh the land," that would have been prose, would it not? There isn't any hint of magic to it that way, is there? "But what *old other* joys outweigh the land" is quite another matter. Here you have all the ringing of the vowels. Over and over again take a line like that and tell a child what it *is*—not what it *means* but what it *is*. Because children will latch on to phrases, particularly (albeit unconsciously) to phrases in which the word order is distinctive. This "every word was once a poem" idea is very real to children. To them old words are not yet stale and new words are exciting. They are to me. A long time ago I first saw the word "docent," which comes from the Latin *docens*—present participle of "teach"—and which in the seventeenth century meant a teacher and is today in Germany combined in *Privatdozent*. But when I saw "docent" for the first time, I thought immediately of the phrase "the decent docent." I don't know why; it was just the pleasant sound of the words. I wrote it down and fairly soon I had four lines:

HISTORY OF EDUCATION

The decent docent doesn't doze:
He teaches standing on his toes.
His student dassn't doze—and does,
And that's what teaching is and was.[11]

Then we should also show children the power of monosyllables. Once, just because I was curious about it, I went through Robert Frost's selected poems in the Penguin edition, and I found that sixty-nine of his poems there begin with a monosyllabic line and that forty-seven of them end with one. You can think of

[11] David McCord (ed.), *What Cheer* (New York: Coward-McCann, Inc., 1945), p. 372.

dozens elsewhere. Shakespeare's *Measure for Measure:* "Aye, but to die, and go we know not where," is only one.[12] But look in Frost—"We love the things we love for what they are."[13] That's the fifteenth line of "Hyla Brook." He meant "Hyla Brook" to be a sonnet, I feel sure, but he found himself with that great line at the end, and naturally it stood. "Whose woods these are, I think I know."[14] "The land was ours before we were the land's"[15] and "Home is the place where, when you have to go there,/They have to take you in."[16] Or a great line of E. L. Mayo, about El Greco's mystical house of the spirit, the radiance outside of it, the shadowy figures going in and out—a symbol of death and the other world. One or two earlier monosyllabic lines contribute to the strength of the poem, but into his last line of ten monosyllables Mayo has written *finis* to the sound of a hammer on white-hot metal: "Why does no light shine through as those doors close?"[17]

Let me say something about the economy of words above the economy of syllables—not only economy but the rare gift of putting simple words together, simple words in a new pattern and in a new thought. This was what Emily Dickinson achieved, not only in her poems, but sometimes (in a more surprising way) in her letters. Nobody

else on earth could have written the following: "I send a violet for L. I should have sent a stem but was overtaken by snowdrifts. I regret deeply not to add a butterfly, but have lost my hat which precludes my catching one."[18] If I could write music for a brass choir, I would take that for a theme.

Finally, there is the matter of humor in verse. The poet writing for children should be sure of his own humor and be at pains to make the reader understand that individual words have humor in them. Light verse to me—if I may stretch a metaphor—is one of the opening doors for children. Take Richard Armour in four lines called "Going to Extremes": "Shake and shake / The catsup bottle, / None will come, / And then a lot'll."[19] Any child can understand that, though it was not written for children. It takes a long while to learn how to be that brief. Here is Armour's "Inscription for a Fly Swatter":

> The hand is quicker than the eye is,
> But somewhat slower than the fly is.[20]

Let me try out four new lines of my own, a quotation in two languages, where the French is very simple; one person speaking to another:

INNUENDO

> You are French? *Je suis.*
> You speak French? *Mais oui.*
> I don't speak French. *Non?*
> I speak English. *Bon!*[21]

[12] William Shakespeare, *Measure for Measure,* Act III, scene 1.

[13] Robert Frost, *Complete Poems* (New York: Holt, Rinehart & Winston, 1949), p. 149.

[14] *Ibid.,* "Stopping By Woods On a Snowy Evening," p. 275.

[15] *Ibid.,* "The Gift Outright," p. 467.

[16] *Ibid.,* "The Death of the Hired Man," p. 53.

[17] Edward Leslie Mayo, "El Greco I," *The Diver* (Minneapolis: University of Minnesota Press, 1947), p. 20.

[18] *Letters of Emily Dickinson,* ed. Mabel Loomis Todd (Boston: Roberts Bros., 1894), **2,** 422 (1885).

[19] From *Light Armour* by Richard Armour. Copyright 1954 by Richard Armour. McGraw-Hill Book Company. Used by permission.

[20] *Ibid.*

[21] From *All Day Long,* copyright © 1965, 1966, by David McCord, with permission of Little, Brown and Company.

That might catch a child somehow; I hope it will. There is a man in England, F. H. Townsend, who took Wordsworth's line "O cuckoo, shall I call thee bird or but a wandering voice?" and added to it so it is now:

O cuckoo, shall I call thee bird, or but a wandering voice?
State the alternative preferred with reasons for your choice.[22]

And then there's Howard Nemerov, who wrote this couplet about a poet whose first book the critics had pulled apart:

A SACRIFICED AUTHOR

Father, he cried, after the critics' chewing,
Forgive them, for they know not what I'm doing.[23]

Here is a parody by Keith Preston of Henley's two most famous lines:

AN AWFUL RESPONSIBILITY

I am the captain of my soul;
I rule it with stern joy;
And yet I think I had more fun,
When I was cabin boy.[24]

The next few poems are included in May Hill Arbuthnot's *Time for Poetry*.[25] I prefer this collection to most of its rivals: large but discriminating. It offers a cluster, to begin with, from the work of Elizabeth Madox Roberts, who wrote *Under the Tree*,[26] a Viking book in print for nearly forty years. Miss Roberts comes nearest of all children's poets to being the child of whom she writes *as she writes*. You remember the firefly one?

FIREFLY

A Song

A little light is going by,
Is going up to see the sky,
A little light with wings.

I never could have thought of it,
To have a little bug all lit
And made to go on wings.[27]

How miraculous is that one for simplicity! Note the use of *could;* not *should* or *would,* but *could.* Here's another one of her poems, about hens:

THE HENS

The night was coming very fast;
It reached the gate as I ran past.

The pigeons had gone to the tower of the church
And all the hens were on their perch,

Up in the barn, and I thought I heard
A piece of a little purring word.

I stopped inside, waiting and staying,
To try to hear what the hens were saying.

They were asking something, that was plain,
Asking it over and over again.

One of them moved and turned around,
Her feathers made a ruffled sound,

A ruffled sound, like a bushful of birds,
And she said her little asking words.

She pushed her head close into her wing,
But nothing answered anything.[28]

My next choice is "Surprise" by Harry Behn:

Our uncle called us on the phone
And Plunky answered all alone,

[22] F. H. Townsend, "To the Cuckoo," in Fougasse (ed.), *An Animal Anthology* (London: Methuen, 1954), p. 117.

[23] *The Next Room of the Dream* (Chicago: University of Chicago Press, 1962), p. 56.

[24] From *Pot Shots from Pegasus* by Keith Preston, © 1957 by Crown. Used by permission of Crown Publishers, Inc.

[25] Chicago: Scott, Foresman & Co., 1952.

[26] Elizabeth Madox Roberts, *Under the Tree* (New York: Viking Press, 1930).

[27] From *Under the Tree* by Elizabeth Madox Roberts. Copyright 1922 by B. W. Huebsch, Inc., 1950 by Ivor S. Roberts. Reprinted by permission of The Viking Press, Inc.

[28] *Ibid.*

And when he asked what she would like
For a surprise, a motor bike?
Or maybe something nice to wear,
A bit of ribbon for her hair?
Or else a pet, perhaps a pair
Of poodle puppies? or a bear?
Or something she might like to do,
Fly to the moon? or tie her shoe?
Or beat him in a game of chess?
All Plunky answered him was, Yes.[29]

Or look at Marchette Chute, whose verse is lighter and less poignant than that of Elizabeth Madox Roberts; but again it is the child herself speaking. Here is "Drinking Fountain":

When I climb up
  To get a drink,
It doesn't work
  The way you'd think.

I turn it up.
  The water goes
And hits me right
  Upon the nose.

I turn it down
  To make it small
And don't get any
  Drink at all.[30]

How good that is for simple observation. Likewise this other one of hers, called "Spring Rain," which is swifter and totally uncontrived:

The storm came up so very quick
  It couldn't have been quicker.
I should have brought my hat along,
  I should have brought my slicker.

My hair is wet, my feet are wet,
  I couldn't be much wetter.
I fell into a river once
  But this is even better.[31]

Another good anthology that reached my shambled desk a short while ago is called *Reflections on a Gift of Watermelon Pickle*.[32] Here is a sample from it called "The Garden Hose" by Beatrice Janosco.

In the gray evening
I see a long green serpent
With its tail in the dahlias

It lies in loops across the grass
And drinks softly at the faucet

I can hear it swallow.[33]

To close with, here are some verses of my own. The opening one is from *Far and Few*, the first of my three books of verse for children. It is one of five chants, so-called; but in the anthologies it has the title, "Every Time I Climb a Tree."

Every time I climb a tree
Every time I climb a tree
Every time I climb a tree
I scrape a leg
Or skin a knee
And every time I climb a tree
I find some ants
Or dodge a bee
And get the ants
All over me

And every time I climb a tree
Where have you been?
They say to me
But don't they know that I am free
Every time I climb a tree?
I like it best
To spot a nest
That has an egg
Or maybe three

[29] From *Wizard in the Well*, copyright © 1956 by Harry Behn. Reprinted by permission of Harcourt, Brace & World, Inc.

[30] Copyright, 1946, by Marchette Chute. From the book *Around and About* by Marchette Chute, published 1957 by E. P. Dutton & Co., Inc., and reprinted with their permission.

[31] Copyright, 1946, by Marchette Chute. From the book *Around and About* by Marchette Chute, published 1957 by E. P. Dutton & Co., Inc., and reprinted with their permission.

[32] Stephen Dunning, Edward Lueders, and Hugh Smith (eds.), *Reflections on a Gift of Watermelon Pickle* (Chicago: Scott, Foresman & Co., 1966).

[33] *Ibid.*, p. 110. Reprinted by permission of Beatrice Janosco.

And then I skin
The other leg
But every time I climb a tree
I see a lot of things to see
Swallows rooftops and TV
And all the fields and farms there be
Every time I climb a tree
Though climbing may be good for ants
It isn't awfully good for pants
But still it's pretty good for me
Every time I climb a tree.[34]

Next is "The Pickety Fence"—another of those five chants. I wrote it in 1924 and sold it to the *Ladies' Home Journal* twenty-five years later, when they were paying six dollars a line. And since four of these lines consist of but one word, I received the highest amount per word I shall ever hope for.

The pickety fence
The pickety fence
Give it a lick it's
The pickety fence
Give it a lick it's
A clickety fence
Give it a lick it's
A lickety fence
Give it a lick
Give it a lick
Give it a lick
With a rickety stick
Pickety
Pickety
Pickety
Pick[35]

Ninety-six dollars!

Here is "Tiger Lily"—an early and quite serious small observation, in which one image (the word reversal of "velvet pretty") seems (and is intended) to dominate:

The tiger lily is a panther,
Orange to black spot:
Her tongue is the velvet pretty anther,
And she's in the vacant lot.

The cool day lilies grow beside her,
But they are done now and dead,
And between them a little silver spider
Hangs from a thread.[36]

A very simple observation. But the point is, suppose I had said "her tongue is the pretty velvet anther"? The whole thing would have gone into the waste basket.

"Cocoon" is a five-line verse on the life cycle of the butterfly. I am rather proud of its compression and sorry that in the *New Yorker* I gave it the trivial title of "Sing Cocoon."

The little caterpillar creeps
Awhile before in silk it sleeps.
It sleeps awhile before it flies,
And flies awhile before it dies,
And that's the end of three good tries.[37]

In "Conversation" a little girl has to go to bed and doesn't want to.

"Mother, may I stay up tonight?"
"No, dear."
"Oh dear! (She always says 'No, dear').
But Father said I might."
"No, dear."
"He did, that is, if you thought it right."
"No, dear, it isn't right."
"Oh dear! Can I keep on the light?"
"No, dear. In spite
Of what your Father said,
You go to bed,
And in the morning you'll be bright
And glad instead
For one more day ahead."
"I might,

[34] "Every Time I Climb a Tree," copyright 1952 by David McCord, from *Far and Few*, with permission of Little, Brown and Company.

[35] "The Pickety Fence," copyright 1952 by David McCord, from *Far and Few*, with permission of Little, Brown and Company.

[36] "Tiger Lily," copyright 1934 by Charles Scribner's Sons, from *Far and Few* by David McCord, with permission of Little, Brown and Company.

[37] "Cocoon," copyright 1949 by The New Yorker, Inc., from *Far and Few* by David McCord, with permission of Little, Brown and Company.

But not for one more night."
"No, dear—*no*, dear."
"At least I've been polite, I guess."
"Yes, dear, you've been polite—
Good night."
"Oh dear,
I'd rather stay down here—
I'm quite . . ."
"No, dear. Now, out of sight."
("Well that was pretty near—")
"*Good* night."
("—all right.")
"Good *night!*"[38]

Two or three very brief ones now. These are silly ones. The first:

> Even though
>   a cat has a kitten,
>   not a rat has a ritten,
>   not a bat a bitten . . .

and on and on. I usually stop the verse at that point and ask all hands (all children's hands) for another rhyme for *cat:* specifically for an animal, fish, insect, or bird. Most of the time at least one hand comes up with *gnat.* So I repeat the verse and add a line. Then I ask them for another one. I suggest a fish. No one knows *sprat,* at which point I may become desperate and say, "Doesn't *anybody* know another rhyme for *cat?*" A little boy holds up his hand and says *dog.* I assume he is lost to poetry.

SCAT! SCITTEN!

> Even though
>   a cat has a kitten,
>   not a rat has a ritten,
>   not a bat has a bitten,
>   not a gnat has a gnitten,
>   not a sprat has a spritten.
>   That is that—that is thitten.[39]

Then I ask them if they know any rhymes for *ladybug.* Yes: *hug, mug, rug, jug.* "No," I explain: "*ladybug* is *three* syllables." There isn't any rhyme for it, of course, so I pretend this time to become desperate again, and a little boy holds up his hand and says *goldfish.* He is *surely* lost. Then I say the verse called "I Want You to Meet . . ." This is for the very young indeed:

I WANT YOU TO MEET . . .

> . . . Meet Ladybug,
> her little sister Sadiebug,
> her mother, Mrs. Gradybug,
> her aunt, that nice oldmaidybug,
> and Baby—she's a fraidybug.[40]

Next is a Christmas poem, a serious one.

COME CHRISTMAS

You see this Christmas tree all silver gold?
It stood out many winters in the cold,

with tinsel sometimes made of crystal ice,
say once a winter morning—maybe twice.

More often it was trimmed by fallen snow
so heavy that the branches bent, with no

one anywhere to see how wondrous is
the hand of God in that white world of his.

And if you think it lonely through the night
when Christmas trees in houses take the light,

remember how his hand put up one star
in this same sky so long ago afar.

All stars are hung so every Christmas tree
has one above it. Let's go out and see.[41]

The poem is a very simple one; but of course all you have to do is stand where a star is visible at 40° or so above the horizon and you've got it.

[38] "Conversation," copyright 1952 by David Mc-Cord, with permission of Little, Brown and Company.

[39] From *Take Sky,* copyright © 1961, 1962, by David McCord, with permission of Little, Brown and Company.

[40] From *Take Sky,* copyright © 1961, 1962, by David McCord, with permission of Little, Brown and Company.

[41] From *All Day Long,* copyright © 1965, 1966, by David McCord, with permission of Little, Brown and Company.

Here is one about piles and piles of pumpkins every New England fall displayed by the filling stations—hundreds and thousands of pumpkins:

PUMPKINS

October sun for miles and miles and miles;
and we were passing piles and piles and piles
of pumpkins—pumpkin-like, so like each other
no pumpkin knew one pumpkin from his
  brother.
If they were carved and placed in aisles and
  aisles,
with piles and piles of smiles and smiles and
  smiles
for miles and miles and miles on some dark
  night,
and one could handle, candle them, and light
the whole creation with Jack Pumpkinheads,
they'd be no wiser. What a pumpkin dreads
is being so conspicuous with eyes
and nose and mouth. Much better off in pies,
say pumpkins. So for miles and miles and
  miles,
with piles of pumpkins—aisles and aisles of
  piles—
just putting all their pumpkinheads together,
you couldn't tell what they were thinking:
  whether
they thought of Halloween, or where they grew
in yellow pumpkin fields. I'd say the view
was pleasing to those pumpkins at the top—
which were of course the best ones in the crop.
But since they had no eyes nowise to know,
they might as well have been down there
  below;
nor could they guess that mile on mile on mile
some boy was hoping he might see one smile.[42]

I shall close with two poems. The first is called "Rapid Reading." A small child has misheard these two words as "rabbit reading" when her mother said them over the telephone. Two little girls talk, and the older sister says to the younger:

"A course in Rabbit Reading?"

"That's what she said. And something else like 'Addled Education.' "

"Rabbits? They can't read. You *know* they can't."

"The one in *Alice* could. At least he had a watch and told the time. And on the front door of his little house—remember?—there was a bright brass plate with w. RABBIT on it. I guess he could read *that*. Perhaps he couldn't spell out WHITE. Which shows . . ."

"*Alice* is a book. Look: Rabbits just don't read. They *breed*. She must have said 'Of course, in rabbit breeding . . .' "

"She didn't, though. She said *a* course in *Rabbit Reading*. Why? We haven't any rabbits that I know of."

"You should have asked her."

"She was on the phone with Mrs. Marples. She's still there on the phone with Mrs. Marples. I also heard her say 'Well lettuce, by all means.' What's *addled* anyway?"

"Just nuts, you nut. But *lettuce*? Did she laugh?"

"No."

"Gee, that's funny."[43]

And now "The Walnut Tree." This poem took me more than fifty years to write, because the event behind it occurred when I was a boy. I was out with my mother, my grandmother, and my uncle in southwestern Pennsylvania, looking at an abandoned farm. While they were off out of sight somewhere, I found this great old walnut tree on the edge of the hill. The tree had a swing with the tallest ropes I ever saw, and the ropes were in pretty good shape. So I took a try, and it swung me right out over the valley. The sight of that valley has haunted me ever since; but

[42] From *All Day Long*, copyright © 1965, 1966, by David McCord, with permission of Little, Brown and Company.

[43] From *All Day Long*, copyright © 1965, 1966, by David McCord, with permission of Little, Brown and Company.

of course I was likewise haunted by Stevenson. Oh, how I liked to go up in a swing, yet I did not want to do it his way. I loved Stevenson as a small boy, but this was my swing, not his. So for years I would think about that experience and even trot out pencil and paper in expectation of an idea. But I never wrote a line, good or bad. Then one day, summer before last, I was driving through a dismal part of Lynn, Massachusetts, when a red light stopped me. And right in the red light I saw the poem, took out my pad and pen and wrote the first few lines, went through the green light, pulled up and wrote ten or twelve more, went home and finished it as fast as that. This is what the deep subconscious can do for you. Here is the poem:

THE WALNUT TREE

There was once a swing in a walnut tree,
As tall as double a swing might be,

At the edge of the hill where the branches spread
So it swung the valley right under me;
Then down and back as the valley fled.
I wonder if that old tree is dead?

I could look straight up in the lifting heart
Of the black old walnut there and start
My flying journey from green to blue
With a wish and a half that the ropes would part
And sail me out on a course as true
As the crows in a flock had dared me to.

I swung from the past to the far dim days
Forever ahead of me. Through the haze
I saw the steeple, a flash of white,
And I gave it a shout for the scare and praise
Of being a boy on the verge of flight.
And I pumped on the swing with all my might

Till the valley widened. Oh, I could guess
From the backward No to the forward Yes
That the world begins in the sweep of eye,
With the wonder of all of it more or less
In the last hello and the first goodbye.
And a swing in the walnut tree is why.[44]

[44] From *All Day Long,* copyright © 1965, 1966, by David McCord, with permission of Little, Brown and Company.

A DEVELOPMENTAL ANALYSIS OF CHILDREN'S RESPONSES TO HUMOR

KATHARINE H. KAPPAS

THE problem of the differing responses of adults and children to humor is an important one in evaluating literature for children. An understanding of these differences may be obtained through a study of the nature, meaning, and developmental formation of a sense of humor and of the factors influencing the individual expression of the humorous attitude. From this analysis the considerations that must be taken into account in an evaluation of humorous children's literature become apparent.

What is meant by the words "humor" and "sense of humor," and what is the relationship between them and laughter?

Arthur Jersild describes laughter as an expressive reaction, not a distinct emotion; as such it may be the release of either negative or positive emotions, and in the release of negative emotions, such as hate or jealousy, it may be seen to reflect a positive attitude.[1] Furthermore, as the diversity of human nature dictates differing degrees of expressive behavior, the presence or absence of laughter does not always indicate the perception of humor in a given situation.[2]

If laughter is an expressive reaction, then what is a sense of humor? A sense of humor can best be defined as an attitude, the attitude of amusement with which an individual meets and interprets a given situation, and it may, as with laughter, be bound up with negative or positive emotions. It has in common with laughter the characteristic of being an affective reaction, but, whereas laughter is a singular overt expressive response, a sense of humor is rather an attitude of amusement intrinsic to the individual and finds numerous forms of expression.

In the discussion that follows the words "humor" and "humorous" refer to situations that amuse, whether they elicit laughter or not, whether they are generated by comedy, wit, or life's absurdities, and whether they are based on negative or positive feelings.[3] Furthermore, humorous situations must have within them an element of incongruity, the association of incompatibles, for them to be perceived as humorous. Incongruity, then, is the basis of all forms of humor though it pervades each one with differing degrees of emphasis. The perception or creation of incongruities can reside within both the emotional and the intellectual spheres, and the incongruous combination of different emotions, objects, situations, and concepts produces a number of major categories of humorous situations which are best described by the element with-

[1] Arthur T. Jersild, "Emotional Development," in Leonard Carmichael (ed.), *Manual of Child Psychology* (2d ed.; New York: John Wiley & Sons, 1954), p. 902.

[2] N. F. Stump, "Sense of Humor and Its Relationship to Personality, Scholastic Aptitude, Emotional Maturity, Height and Weight," *Journal of General Psychology,* 20 (1939), 25.

[3] Katharine Hull Kappas, "A Study of Humor in Children's Books" (unpublished M.A. dissertation, University of Chicago, 1965), p. 43.

in each most emphasized to achieve the humorous effect. Obviously, the more elements combined within a humorous situation, the more complex it becomes.[4]

The following is a suggested list of categories of humor, or humorous situations, compiled for an analysis of humorous juvenile literature from studies done by a number of investigators of children's humor; an examination of this list readily indicates the great diversity of the sources of humor.

CATEGORIES OF HUMOR[5]

1. *Exaggeration,* making use primarily of an obvious over- or understatement of such things as size, numbers, proportions, facts, feelings, deeds, experiences, etc.
2. *Incongruity,* associating two generally accepted incompatibles; it is the lack of a rational relation of objects, people, or ideas to each other or to the environment.
3. *Surprise,* exploiting the occurrence of the unexpected—whether fact, thought, feeling, or event; in its more sophisticated form it becomes *irony.*
4. *Slapstick,* the form of humor that depends for its effect on fast, boisterous, and zany physical activity and horseplay . . . often accompanied by broad obvious rowdy verbal humor.
5. *The absurd,* that which obviously lacks reason, which is foolish or ridiculous in its lack of good sense, includes *nonsense,* the nonsensical use of logic and language; the *preposterous,* arising from the incongruity of reality and fantasy; and *whimsy,* a fanciful or fantastic device, object, or creation especially in writing, art, or decoration.
6. *Human predicaments,* featuring situations in which a character appears foolish or bested, includes the humor of *superiority* and *degradation,* which is based on self-aggrandizement or the release of hostility through the discomfiture, failure, or misfortune of others, and *comic predicaments,* which is based on an attitude of sympathetic acceptance of the human predicament and can be seen in situations in which either oneself or someone else appears foolish or bested by life for the moment; in this case, however, no hostile feelings are intended to be aroused or expressed.
7. *Ridicule,* primarily the teasing and mockery of others or oneself, can be seen expressed, for example, in the mockery of adults, their bigness, power, foibles, their world and its customs and institutions, etc. *Negative ridicule* finds its source in feelings of self-aggrandizement or the release of hostility through the mockery of others. *Playful ridicule,* on the other hand, is based on the sympathetic acceptance of human foibles. *Satire* is primarily a sophisticated artistic form of humor arising from both types of ridicule.
8. *Defiance,* primarily the release of hostility or aggression through rebellion, includes the violation of conventions, the perpetration of situations socially unacceptable to adults, the expression of forbidden ideas, and the violation of adult authority.
9. *Violence,* primarily the release of hostility or aggression through the

[4] *Ibid.,* pp. 44–45.

[5] *Ibid.,* Categories of Humor, Table 2, pp. 53–56.

expression of sudden or extreme violence.

10. *Verbal humor,* the manipulation of language through word play, puns, jokes, sarcasm, wit, name-calling, and the like, may contain either a positive or negative emotional content but differs from the other forms in being a verbal rather than a situational form of humor.

Given these definitions of humor and laughter and the categorical listing of forms of humor, the next consideration is a theory and description of the formation of the individual's sense of humor and the factors influencing both the evident diversity among individuals of the same age and experience and the frequent disparities between the humorous behavior of children and adults.

How does a child's sense of humor come into being? Considerable evidence supports the view that the formation of a sense of humor follows a general developmental pattern and that this pattern parallels and is dependent upon the child's intellectual and emotional development.[6] The intellectual perception of humor within a given situation demands a familiarity with the elements within the situation and a comprehension of their normal relationships. One must know what is normal before being able to perceive an incongruity. As Jersild points out, the child appreciates incongruities of size and space only after he is familiar with normal relationships between objects.[7] His comprehension and expression of verbal humor follow a mastery of language and grow only at the rate that it does.

This is equally true with respect to his emotional development and his capacity for the expression of humor, because a certain maturity is required before the child becomes fully responsive to his own emotional environment.[8] For most children the accumulation of experiences brings a heightened awareness of their feelings and strivings and an increased sensitivity to the complexities of situations and relationships.[9] As the child becomes increasingly able to perceive himself objectively in ever more complex situations, he will be able, when necessary, to perceive the humor of his own predicament in these situations. The over-all pattern is one of a progressive expansion of the child's sense of humor into more and more areas of emotional and intellectual experience until he becomes increasingly adept at utilizing humor for his own ends.

There are some general trends which are evident in the formation of children's humor. First, for the average child a sense of humor develops on a progressive though intermittent course. At some periods in the child's life it would seem that he had lost the sense of humor which he had developed up to that moment; but after the passage of a little time it returns and appears on yet another level of understanding. Further, as a child matures his humorous behavior becomes increasingly more individual. A group of first graders will evidence a much greater degree of homogeneity in their perception of humor, for example, than a comparable group

[6] *Ibid.,* pp. 6–39.

[7] Arthur T. Jersild, *Child Psychology* (5th ed.; Englewood Cliffs, N.J.: Prentice-Hall, Inc., 1960), pp. 250–54.

[8] Florence Justin, "A Genetic Study of Laughter-Provoking Stimuli," *Child Development,* 3 (1932), 131.

[9] Kappas, *op. cit.,* p. 20.

of high school children.[10] And, finally, visual forms of humor generally dominate until the child reaches high school, when verbal humor and wit begin to command increasing attention and gradually become the major forms of humorous behavior.[11]

Obviously, the formation of an individual's sense of humor is not solely dependent on a developmental sequence but on other factors as well. The opinion of most investigators is that the greatest diversity in perception and expression of humor can be found between individuals rather than between groups.[12]

Previous studies have revealed several factors that appear to explain the differing levels and characteristics of individual humorous attitudes. Sex is one determinant; not only do boys and girls on the whole fail to find the same things funny to the same degree, but they will often classify humorous situations differently. This sex difference increases with age.[13]

There also appears to be a positive correlation between an individual's intelligence and his sense of humor. The more intelligent person is able to perceive a greater variety of humorous situations than his intellectually less able peer. And the degree of intelligence also influences the individual's preference with respect to forms and expression of humor.[14]

The cultural background of an individual is also seen to influence his preference for and appreciation of humor. Ruth Wells's study, for example, indicated that pupils in "the school of higher cultural level showed greater appreciation for satire and whimsy and less taste for slapstick and absurdity than did . . . the pupils in corresponding grades in schools of lower cultural level."[15]

Personality is yet another factor that influences an individual's humorous attitude. Personality differences help to account not only for the variation in the humorous expressive behavior of people but also for their diverse tastes in humor. Landis and Ross in their study on "Humor and Its Relation to Other Personality Traits" found a distinct difference, for example, in the humorous preferences of introverts and extroverts.[16]

Therefore, a composite of an individual's personality, sex, education, intelligence, emotional maturity, and experience determines the humorous attitude and accounts for the substantial differences in appreciation of humor among individuals regardless of age. However, in any analysis of children's humor one is consciously or unconsciously thinking in terms of children's humor as opposed to adult humor. Therefore, in this context, it is the developmental se-

[10] Leo Graham, "The Maturational Factor in Humor," *Journal of Clinical Psychology,* **14** (1958), 326–28.

[11] Ernest Harms, "The Development of Humor," *Journal of Abnormal and Social Psychology,* **38**, No. 3 (July, 1943), 357; Alexander Laing, "The Sense of Humor in Childhood and Adolescence," *British Journal of Educational Psychology,* **9** (1939), 201.

[12] Kappas, *op. cit.,* p. 46.

[13] Carney Landis and John W. H. Ross, "Humor and Its Relation to Other Person-Personality Traits," *Journal of Social Psychology,* **4** (1933), 156–75.

[14] *Ibid.;* L. Mones, "Intelligence and a Sense of Humor," *Journal of the Exceptional Child,* **5** (1939), 150–53.

[15] Ruth E. Wells, "A Study of Tastes in Humorous Literature among Pupils of Junior and Senior High Schools," *Journal of Educational Research,* **28** (1934), 88.

[16] Landis and Ross, *op. cit.,* 156–75.

quence of humor that is of importance to us.

The distinctive role that maturity and age play in the formation of a child's sense of humor can be seen in a comparison of the attitudes toward humor of the child at different age levels. What the child is interested in and familiar with and how he views himself and his world determine the content and the level of his sense of humor at each age. The following are brief developmental profiles of the child and his sense of humor at ages, five, nine, and fourteen, drawn from Gesell's work and from other research.[17]

THE FIVE YEAR OLD

The five year old is a fairly well integrated child both physically and emotionally. He appears content and contained much of the time. In spite of the fact that he has started kindergarten, his world is composed mostly of the "here-and-now,"[18] of his mother and his home life. His thoughts and play are directed toward his home, and as he plays he works at making all that is already familiar to him even more so. He is consolidating all that he learned and experienced in the previous years and makes no real effort to expand his world beyond his home and family.

For this child the world is himself. Although he may play with other children in small groups, he is not really aware of them as unique individuals but is primarily involved with his own private world. "He is so completely immersed in the cosmos that he is unaware of his own thinking as being a subjective process separate from the objective world."[19]

With no capacity as yet to think in abstract terms, his comprehension of space and time is confined to the moment at hand. The average five-year-old child is just beginning to learn numbers and letters and to take delight in manipulating them as they become familiar. Furthermore, "his thinking processes are so subjective and concrete that abstract thoughts and ideas of truth and honesty are beyond his comprehension."[20]

Much of the five year old's humor is provoked by his own motor activity, his physical posturing and play. He delights in slapstick humor. The types of situations that elicit amusement revolve around the socially unacceptable—unacceptable within his frame of reference. He also responds to anything strange or unusual, including misery and despair, thinking them funny or amusing. A "social smile," simple in itself, may evoke amusement, as will the elements of "surprise" and "incongruity," all of which must be operative within the framework of his familiar world to be comprehensible and thus amusing to him.[21]

This child who is beginning to understand the relationship of objects and sizes and learning his numbers as well will find much humor in the exaggeration of each of these. The use of exaggeration is not limited to objects but may include the magnification of violence to the point of the preposterous.

Just as he likes to manipulate sizes

[17] Arnold Gesell and Frances L. Ilg, *The Child from Five to Ten* (New York: Harper & Bros., 1946); Arnold Gesell, Frances Ilg, and Louise Bates Ames, *Youth: The Years from Ten to Sixteen* (New York: Harper & Bros., 1956); and Kappas, *op. cit.*

[18] Gesell and Ilg, *op. cit.*, p. 63.

[19] *Ibid.*, p. 66.

[20] Kappas, *op. cit.*, p. 28.

[21] Justin, *op. cit.*, p. 130.

and numbers with which he has become familiar, so will he start to take pleasure in an elementary form of word play. His expression of verbal humor is dependent entirely on the words he knows and most often is seen in simple riddles or in play with proper names.

THE NINE YEAR OLD

The nine year old is a highly self-motivated child who delights in spending much time perfecting physical and intellectual skills which may fascinate him. He can often be found repeating over and over various tasks until he feels absolutely confident that he fully understands and has mastered them.

Moving from the five year old's subjective immersion of self in a family environment to a world that has expanded to include his school, his friends, his clubs, and social groups within his community, in each of which he views himself as a part of a group, the nine year old explores his personal relationships with some degree of objectivity. He is interested in other people and is fairly adept at appraising and criticizing himself and others, although the ramifications of such appraisals may be somewhat lost on him. The awakening of "elementary ideas of justice,"[22] of an individual conscience, and the comprehension of the abstract ethical concepts of truth and honesty are becoming evident. They are sporadic in appearance and performance and seem rather simple in form, but they are beginning to take root and grow. In every instance the nine year old is seeking to find a place for himself, and as he does so there is an expansion and growth of his emotional capacity.

This increased individuality and the search for individual status find expression in the nine year old's perception and expression of humor. Far less homogeneity of humor is found among the nine year olds than among five-year-old children. The perseverance in a task or thought, evident in their other behavior, is also present in their discernment of the amusing.[23] If something strikes them as funny, they will repeat it with the same feeling of delight at each repetition.

The nine year old still appreciates some of the same types of humor as the five year old. However, not only has his appreciation intensified but the humorous situations themselves have become much finer in form and content. Much as one would expect, his verbal humor is increasing, and he now partakes in the ready-made moron jokes so old and familiar, in puns, and in more complicated riddles.

The humor of these children may also reveal some hostility and aggression, for, not only do they enjoy behavior or situations of which adults disapprove and sometimes delight in the misfortunes of others, but they also find amusement in deviations from the normal and conventional.[24] The expression of taboo subjects increasingly finds an outlet in humor as the child matures, and the joking forms of the nine year old show this.

The degree of "self-objectification"[25] this child has achieved over the five year old permits him occasionally to accept jokes about himself expressed by others. Most of the time, however, it is

[22] Gesell and Ilg, op. cit., p. 191.

[23] Kappas, op. cit., p. 36.

[24] Jersild, "Emotional Development," p. 903.

[25] G. W. Allport, Pattern and Growth in Personality (New York: Holt, Rinehart & Winston, 1961), p. 293.

touch and go whether he will view such expressions as humorous or catastrophic.

THE FOURTEEN YEAR OLD

The nine year old has his base in the child's world, and, although often trying to reach beyond his years, he is by no means as yet approaching the adult world. The fourteen-year-old child, on the other hand, not only can perceive the difference between his and the adult world, but knows as well that he will soon participate in the latter.

The intellectual differences between the nine and fourteen year old are quite considerable, for by fourteen "two verbal components of human intelligence, namely verbal comprehension and word fluency, . . . mature to four-fifths of the adult level."[26] And from this follows a parallel increase in the child's capacity for logical thinking.[27] This development in intellectual capacity permeates nearly every other aspect of his life. He shows greater ability for critical self-appraisal, for emotional expression, and for the comprehension and integration of abstract concepts.

The development of an ethical code of behavior is a sporadic affair. The child's intellectual comprehension of ethical abstractions seems to precede in some cases the actual integration of the code of behavior into his own pattern responses. His intense interest in fair play goes beyond himself, and he has strong feelings about what is right and wrong; but his conscience still is not always reliable when expressed in personal behavior. He may or may not be honest, depending on whether he feels a strong need to protect himself.

His understanding of time and space has expanded. He now thinks of his life less in immediate terms and more in terms of seasons and years, demonstrating a deepening chronological sense of time.

Although his own world now fully encompasses his home, school, and community and he is able to project himself into the world beyond, he is mostly involved in school life and all that evolves from that experience. In his constant investigation of the world around him he is seeking for his own identity and tries to find it in the activities he pursues and in his interpersonal relationships. The fourteen year old is very absorbed in personal relationships, developing many friendships and partaking in numerous group activities. Grouping is predominantly by sex, but there is some early dating and mixing of boys and girls in groups. He thinks about his friends a great deal, tries to "figure them out," and is learning "to perceive how others feel, and to see himself as others see him."[28]

The fourteen year old's sense of humor reflects the developmental level he has attained. By this age the considerable individual differences in sense of humor which are so evident among adults are already well formed.

The critical analysis and sensitivity with which he approaches his friends and himself has its counterpart in his humorous attitude. There is a growing tendency of the majority to "reflect on why they laugh, and of a minority (especially among the girls) to deprecate laughter that is unfeeling."[29] Sometimes his sense of humor is directed toward his parents or teachers, sometimes his

[26] Gesell, Ilg, and Ames, *op. cit.*, p. 179.

[27] *Ibid.*

[28] *Ibid.*, p. 176.

[29] Laing, *op. cit.*, p. 201.

peers; but he is just as likely to be able to turn his "humor back on himself in a kidding way or express mild, good-natured sarcasm."[30] This child has achieved enough objectivity to be able to laugh at himself occasionally.

Among themselves the fourteen year olds' humorous behavior consists primarily of joking insults, ridicule, and a considerable amount of "loud, 'corny' humor in public places."[31] Practical jokes which were previously very popular are now beginning to lose appeal. Although humor dealing with forbidden ideas and subjects is prevalent, particularly among boys, it is not indulged in in group situations or in mixed company as much as it had been earlier.[32]

Children at this age level generally have definite preferences for certain forms of humorous literature. According to one study, they rank the literature of absurdity first, slapstick second, satire third, and whimsy fourth in appeal. As they grow older there is evidence of an increasing appreciation of satire and whimsy and a slight decrease in the enjoyment of absurdity.[33]

Further, the level of maturity seen in this child's capacity for logical thinking, verbal comprehension, and word fluency finds an outlet in his greater appreciation for verbal wit. From this age on verbal wit and humor will become increasingly dominant.[34]

Discernible in these profiles of children at ages five, nine, and fourteen is the progressive expansion of a child's sense of humor into the extended boundaries of his self-knowledge, his

knowledge of the world, and his increasing emotional and intellectual capacities. It becomes obvious that not only the form of humor is important but the level of the content and the degree of self-involvement demanded by the humorous situation.

The five-year-old child's humor revolves around slapstick, his own motor activity, and the response to a simple social smile. There is evidence of the enjoyment of defiance of parents through situations known to be unacceptable to them. Simple surprise is a great delight, but the humor of irony, where the unexpected is often in mockery of the appropriate and expected, does not achieve its full effect on this child (who will only note the element of surprise). His verbal humor is limited to simple word play and riddles. This child is so involved in himself and his own world that he has no real capacity for sympathetic humor toward himself or others (as seen in the humor of comic predicaments) beyond a play situation, such as "aren't I naughty; see how funny I am," which is in reality a form of innocuous defiance.

The nine-year-old child enjoys many of the same forms of humor as the five year old, but in each case they are much more intensified, diversified, and refined. There is a marked increase in his capacity for verbal humor, and the expression of generally taboo subjects has shown a significant gain. The most notable change, however, is evident in the increased degree of "self-objectification." The result of this is the beginning ability to perceive and create sympathetic humor toward himself and others, to be able to use humor for his own ends, and thus to channel negative feelings into positive humorous situations.

The fourteen year old is poised on the

[30] Gesell, Ilg, and Ames, *op. cit.*, p. 182.

[31] *Ibid.*, p. 345.

[32] *Ibid.*, p. 343.

[33] Wells, *op. cit.*, pp. 81–91.

[34] Laing, *op. cit.*, p. 201.

edge of the adult world, and the level of development of his humor reflects this precarious balance. At this age verbal humor and wit begin to dominate over visual humor for the first time, indicative of the significant gains in his verbal comprehension. Furthermore, what was an incipient sense of humor regarding the frailties of himself and others is beginning to show signs of maturing with the marked increase in his ability for self-appraisal and critical judgment of others. There is, then, a noticeable advance in the use of humor as a conscious vehicle for negative and positive emotions. Thus, the maturing of a sense of humor does indeed parallel an individual's intellectual and emotional development.

EVALUATION

How can the developmental theory of the formation of a sense of humor be applied to the critical evaluation of children's literature?

From the previous discussion it becomes apparent that there are a number of considerations to bear in mind in the evaluation of humorous books for specific age levels. Any critical analysis of this literature should consider three specific factors inherent in a humorous situation which determine the level of comprehension required for its fullest employment: These factors are (1) the form of humor, (2) the level of the intellectual and emotional content and demands of this humorous situation, and (3) the size of the world or the frame of reference of its content. They are expressed in the following questions. (1) Forms of humor: (a) What are the forms of humor employed in the story? (b) Is the humor expressed in simple sequence or does it appear in a complex combination of humorous types?

Obviously, books with either multiple intentions or multiple humorous situations or both are more complex and require a special maturity of perception and comprehension to be fully appreciated. (2) Level of intellectual and emotional content of humorous situations: (a) What is the conceptual level of the content of the humor? Does it deal with abstract concepts or literal objects? (b) How complex is the verbal and logical content of the humorous situation? (c) How complex are the emotional demands of the humorous situation? Does it require a gross or highly differentiated emotional response? (d) How much "self-objectification" is either evident on the part of a literary character or is demanded of the reader? (3) The size of the world: For what age child is the size and scope and material reference of the literary world presented appropriate?

In each case the key point revolves around the questions: Is the child familiar with this material, has he experienced it, and is it appropriate to his intellectual and emotional development at that moment? A discussion of two books that are good examples of stories highly successful in expressing humor appropriate for the specific age level for which they are intended will serve to illustrate this approach to the humor in children's literature.

The Backward Day by Ruth Krauss[35] is a story intended for children five through seven. The essentials of the story are as follows: A small boy wakes up one morning and decides that it is a backward day. He puts all of his clothes on backwards, ending with his underwear over his overcoat, walks down-

[35] Ruth Krauss, *The Backward Day,* illus. Marc Simont (New York: Harper & Bros.).

stairs backwards, goes into the dining room backwards, sits in his chair backwards, and says "good night" instead of "good morning." His parents go along with him and watch as he walks out of the dining room backwards, goes back up the stairs backwards, and gets into bed. Then he hops out of bed and starts the day again, only this time starting at the beginning instead of the end.

This is a story simply constructed around a single humorous episode. The humor results from the little boy's playful defiance of conventional morning behavior. He is in effect saying "Phooey to the grownups' way of doing things" and then in a very logical way reversing the exact order of the day. The child is careful to maintain the precise and orderly reversal of the normal patterns of behavior. The result is a situation that appears to be absurd and silly, although basically one that is built on a straightforward reversed logic.

All of the elements in this story should be familiar to the average child from five to seven. The story takes places in the home; it concerns the conventional morning behavior of how to get up, get dressed, come downstairs, sit at the table, and say "good morning"—all very familiar tasks. Children of this age know what they are supposed to say in the morning and what the correct order of dressing is. They also know that these are adult rules of proper behavior in which they have been schooled for some time. At this age these children relish the great pleasure of doing just the opposite of what adults tell them to do, especially when an act of defiance does not pose a serious threat to them. The humor in this story, then, is very clear and simple,

described by a single episode and a single type of humorous behavior appropriate to the age level for which it is intended. On an action rather than a verbal level, it requires only the perception of the reversal of the ordinary pattern of behavior which adults expect in a very familiar routine. The emotional involvement demanded by the situation is also uncomplex, a simple "I defy you, adult world" in a situation that is not threatening.

Beverly Cleary's book *Henry and Ribsy*[36] is another good example of a story that expresses humor appropriate to the age level for which it is intended, in this case the nine through eleven year olds. The humor results from "Henry and Ribsy's perpetual difficulties, none of which seem to arise from an intentional desire to provoke trouble but rather from an accidental blundering, momentary forgetfulness, or well-intentioned but mistakened actions."[37] All the situations show Henry and Ribsy bested for the moment but carrying the complete sympathy and support of the author and the reader. Nearly all the situations are dependent upon Henry's devotion to his dog, Ribsy, and his family's love and acceptance of the two in spite of their occasional and very human annoyance at the steady round of small troubles that Henry and Ribsy bring them.

The world Miss Cleary creates for Henry and Ribsy is the very world in which the nine-year-old boy is most actively involved, his school, his home, his friends, and neighbors, and his dog if he has one. The fact that in spite of all that happens to Henry he is still

[36] Beverly Cleary, *Henry and Ribsy,* illus. Louis Darling (New York: William Morrow & Co., 1954).

[37] Kappas, *op. cit.,* p. 78.

able to maintain a certain degree of aplomb is also an accurate portrayal of the level of objectivity that children of this age have generally reached. This is not to say that Henry is not upset over the predicaments that Ribsy generates for him; but his unhappiness has a maturity to it that prevents him from going into tantrums or losing hope. This is in keeping with the general developmental level and optimism of the child at this age.

We see, then, that the environment, the content of the humorous situations, and the behavior of the principal character are all suited to the interests and experiences of a child this age. The form of humor dominant here, that of comic predicaments arising out of someone's misfortune and inability to handle situations that may seem simple to the uninvolved, is one of the forms of humor especially appreciated by children of this age. In every respect the humor of this story is appropriate to the age level for which it is intended.

Both *Henry and Ribsy* and *The Backward Day* were written for a single audience with a thematic content and structure permitting only one level of appeal and interpretation. As such the critical evaluation of the humor of these books and others like them is relatively uncomplicated. Books such as *Alice's Adventures in Wonderland*,[38] *The Rescuers*,[39] *Winnie-the-Pooh*,[40] and *The*

Bee-Man of Orn[41] present a much more difficult problem. In each of these books the humor and story are operative on several levels and thus have appeal for a broad age range. Frequently, the appeal these books has for various ages is due not so much to a general sharing of appreciation or interpretation as to the diverse appeals within the same incident and to the multiple levels of experience the literary situation affords. In some instances a child may be found enjoying the plot line, adventure, and fantasy in the situation described, for example, while the adult is enjoying its underlying parody. At other times a child may enjoy the obvious humor in a situation based on a human predicament whereas the adult enjoys the satire inherent in the entire story of which the single situation is only an elaboration.

Therefore, books with multiple levels of appeal must be carefully evaluated to determine the nature of this appeal for the different age levels that will constitute their audience. This is especially important in order to avoid the inappropriate selection of stories for children at a time when the factors for which the stories have been selected may be unappreciated and perhaps result in the future rejection of important and classic examples of literature.

[38] Lewis Carroll, *Alice's Adventures in Wonderland*, illus. Peter Newell (New York: Harper & Bros., 1901).

[39] Margery Sharp, *The Rescuers*, illus. Garth Williams (Boston: Little, Brown & Co., 1959).

[40] A. A. Milne, *Winnie-the-Pooh*, illus. Ernest H. Shepard (New York: E. P. Dutton & Co., 1926).

[41] Frank R. Stockton, *The Bee-Man of Orn*, illus. Maurice Sendak (New York: Holt, Rinehart & Winston, 1964).

MACHINE ANIMISM IN MODERN CHILDREN'S LITERATURE

H. JOSEPH SCHWARCZ

INANIMATE OBJECTS AS PROTAGO-
NISTS—HANS CHRISTIAN
ANDERSEN

LITERATURE of all times and of all peoples has always known and told of man-made objects that took on a magic quality and served their owners in miraculous ways. But inanimate objects as protagonists of tales can be found, before the latter half of the nineteenth century, only very rarely. In order to be the hero of a tale, the object has to undergo a process of animation; it is shaped by technological processes so as to be useful to man, is perceived as an entity, and is endowed with "life"; the leap fantasy has to take is much greater than in the anthropomorphization of talking beasts.

A few examples can be adduced. The old Caucasian (the term being used in its geographical, not its racial, sense) motif of "The kitchen utensils' rebellion against man" tells of excited pots and pans, etc., that will not stand their servitude any more, but the good house-wife finds a way to pacify them. In one version of "The Pot," a Danish folk tale,[1] the story's hero is a pot that wanders from one home to another in the village and endeavors to bring food to the poor. The pot speaks, and replies when spoken to; it shows understand-ing. Yet its owner received it from the hands of a good witch, and it is at her command that he has taken up the task of going from door to door looking for the deserving poor. In another ver-sion of the same tale,[2] it is in a poor man's possession and "skips" to more fortunate homes and farms and steals food, grain, and money for its owner; it talks and acts independently and re-sponds to questions. It was given to its owner by "a fine-faced stranger." The tale bears social significance: it is a kind of Robin Hood pot, but of defi-nitely magical origin.

In Goethe's "Wandering Bell,"[3] the church bell leaves its steeple and har-asses the child who refuses to come to church for Sunday prayers. Yet the child has been forewarned by his mother that this might finally happen; the bell therefore appears to have been sent by some higher power.

The common characteristics of the objects in the tales cited seem to be that, though personified, they appear in stories that are actually parables and that man's superiority is not questioned. And, as has been mentioned, the ex-amples are relatively rare.

All this was changed by the appear-ance of the first writer of modern fan-tasy, Hans Christian Andersen. His unusually sensitive mind discovered life in everyone and everything; what-ever his fantasy touched upon became for him the bearer of a destiny, the

[1] "Der Topf" (Dänemark), *Europäische Volks-marchen,* ausgewalt von Max Luthy (Zurich: Manesse: Bibliothek der Weltliteratur, 1951), pp. 51–57.

[2] "The Talking Pot," *Thirteen Danish Tales,* re-told by Mary C. Hatch (New York: Harcourt, Brace & Co., 1947), pp. 16–24.

[3] Johann Wolfgang Goethe, "Die Wandlende Glocke," *Goethe's Gedichte* (Berlin: Verlag der Literaturwerke "Minerva," n.d.), p. 83.

symbol of the pervading sadness and happiness he saw all around him, and the vehicle for his intensely human message.

Andersen's animation of man-made objects manifests itself in various ways. Some of the stories are frankly allegorical. "The Shirt Collar,"[4] a would-be Don Juan, conducts unhappy love affairs with several female objects—the garter, the hot iron, a scissors, and a comb. When he gets old, he—like Casanova before him—retells his adventures in a form embellished by his memory. But other tales create a more emotional atmosphere, calling upon the reader's feelings just as if their heroes were human or animal. "The Old Street Lamp"[5] becomes more and more human as the story develops, and in the end he feels that the old couple whose rooms he brightens are fond of him for his own sake: "I'm really like a child to them." In "The Old House,"[6] one of Andersen's most tranquil and original tales, the old house, the new houses, the little boy, the flowers, the old man, the birds, the brass knobs on the railings, the carved trumpeter, and the tin soldier curiously live side by side in "one world" and even a scrap of pigskin covering "has something to say." One could only with difficulty determine who really is the hero of this story: None of them really stands out, and the general mood, of life passing away from all of us, serves as the great equalizer in this story.

And yet Andersen's animated man-made objects inhabit a strange land. They are alive, so it seems; they are personified and equipped with human attributes; they are conscious of their existence; they contemplate their experiences and become wiser for doing so; they are very sensitive creatures. On the other hand, though, they are wrong in assuming that they are important to man; they are alive, but they are so much wrapped up in their narcissistic memories that they never realize that they are not free to act; they strive for independence but fail to attain it. Their existence is, from man's point of view, a tragic and ridiculous illusion—yet again, they are alive enough to lead their illusory existence. Behind it we can discern Andersen's existentialist view of human life. Man uses his tools and prides himself on them as long as they are new and fit his purposes. As they become dented and cracked they become worthless, and we throw them away. Some of the wiser among the objects are aware that this is so.

The "Tea-Pot"[7] gains more insight into the conditions of existence in this world than any other object. She knows, in spite of her pride in herself, that she is in fact much less important than she would have us believe. As this deeply symbolic tale develops, the suffering tea-pot slowly perceives something of elementary importance—*the superiority of organic substance over the inorganic.* In the hour of her humiliation: "Even as I stood there, my better life began: you are one thing, and then you become something quite different. . . . Earth was put inside me and for a tea-pot that's as much as being buried . . . in the earth a bulb was planted . . . the bulb lay in the earth, the bulb lay inside me." And the tea-pot begins to believe

[4] Han Christian Andersen, *H. C. Andersen's Fairy Tales,* trans. L. W. Kingsland (New York: Henry Z. Walck, Inc., 1962), pp. 309–12. Hereafter referred to as Kingsland edition.

[5] *Ibid.,* pp. 290–98.

[6] *Ibid.,* pp. 299–308.

[7] *Ibid.,* pp. 325–27.

in its own transformation: ". . . it became my heart, my living heart . . .
there was life in me, there was strength
and force."[8] This ecstatic hymn to life
is rudely interrupted when people point
out that the beautiful flower deserves a
better pot. The tea-pot is thrown out
into the yard; yet even there she is
forever ennobled by her illusory experience of organic wholeness and preg-
nancy. In "The Nightingale,"[9] Andersen states even more unequivocally that
the living animal is superior to the arti-
fact.

It is intriguing to speculate on what
drove Andersen to preoccupy himself
so much with the fictional character
and essence of objects. The same forces
that brought about his character and
nourished his imagination possibly also
strengthened this aspect of his mind.

The "pan-animation" found in Andersen's work may be explained as a reaction to, or a projection of, the perpetual
excitement and the abnormally high,
almost paranoid, level of fantasy that
existed in his childhood environment.
His empathy for the lowliest things in
existence—the neck of a broken bottle,
a scrap of pigskin—can be seen as the
expression of compassion by one who
knew what it was to grow up in utter
poverty and who wanted, consciously or
unconsciously, to remind his reader that
even the most neglected object has a
dignity of its own, or at least imagines
so.

In an uncanny way, Andersen moved
creative fantasy ahead toward the animation, in fantasy, of inanimate man-
made objects, exactly at the time when
the influence of the Industrial Revolution was about to alter man's life beyond recognition. It is as if he had

[8] *Ibid.*, pp. 326–27.

[9] *Ibid.*, pp. 172–84.

intuitively, seismographically, understood that mankind, in his own time,
stood on the threshold of a new age
and would soon recast his material environment and, beyond that, would become involved in technological and
psychological attempts to adjust to the
inanimate works of his own creation.

Andersen created the "industrial
revolution" in children's literature, the
animism in modern fantasy. In the
generations following him, man-made
objects have managed to improve their
lot and their relative importance, both
in reality and in the realm of fantasy.

MAGIC OBJECTS AND AUTONOMOUS OBJECTS[10]

From Andersen's stories about animated objects, two main types of children's literature have grown: stories
about animated dolls and toy animals;
and stories about useful and serviceable
objects (tools, gadgets, and machines).

Although dolls and toy animals that
come to life in children's daydreams
and fantasies, and in the fantasy stories
written for them, are man-made objects,
at least they have been created for the
express purpose of serving as objects
to which the child is supposed to become attached; their function is to represent biological beings toward whom
real emotional attachment—love, hate,

[10] In the following sections of this study most of
the examples referred to in the text will be taken
from American research, and literature for children and adults, etc. The reason for this is that
American sources were the most easily accessible
at the time of writing this paper. Another reason
is, of course, the fact that the phenomena dealt
with are to be found in America more than elsewhere, America being the most highly developed
technological society. But examples taken from
other cultures and languages will be introduced to
emphasize the fact that these phenomena are intimately connected with the evolution of technology
and cybernetics and that the problems they pose
are of concern to man and society everywhere.

confidence, admiration, etc.—is possible, or even necessary. They have symbolic significance as vehicles for projection and identification. They are, moreover, the descendants of what Garland calls "the great tradition of anthropomorphism"[11]—the descendants of sacred effigies and statues and images that symbolically represented gods and goddesses in countless cults and, of course, of the toys that children cherished in almost every culture and every generation. And they are, after all, anthropomorphic or theriomorphic—they resemble real creatures who have faces and limbs and personalities. Learning to relate to these real beings, even when they are represented by proxy, is one of the decisive aspects of growing up and of living.

Another no less important point will become manifest through a short survey of the development of the doll and toy animal stories. Arbuthnot[12] and Meigs et al.[13] trace this development through the nineteenth and twentieth centuries and make it clear—without commenting on it—that animation more often than not takes place in an exceptional, often magical, situation or because the child loves his toy so much that his wish comes true. Coming to life is an exceptionally rare experience, as it were, not an ordinary, everyday occurrence. Some of the examples cited by these authors include: Collodi's *Pinocchio*, Margery W. Bianco's *Velveteen Rabbit*, A. A. Milne's *Winnie-the-Pooh*, Elizabeth O. Jones's *Big Susan*, Enys Tregarthen's *The Doll Who Came Alive*.

The fantasy situation adopted by stories of this type is, therefore, one in which the child relates in a psychologically meaningful way to the fantastic creatures of the writers' minds; yet they, the animated toys, usually depend on him and are not his equals. The human child's superiority is—exactly as in animal stories and in the child's relation to his pets—one of the educative values of those relationships because it partly balances and partly compensates for his inferiority feelings toward the adults in his life.

However, the other type—stories about functional, useful artifacts—does not seem to possess these educationally valuable attributes. Here and there one can find objects that belong to a magic world: "And the soup ladle was walking up the table towards Alice's chair, and beckoning to her impatiently to get out of its way."[14] Yet the twentieth century has evolved *stories about man-made objects that are represented as "naturally" active, autonomous in their actions, and co-existing with the child on a basis of equality and even, on occasion, being superior to him.* They share the child's world in a matter-of-fact manner, relate to him and care for him out of their own free will, as it were.

ANTHROPOMORPHIC VEHICLES AND MACHINES

The personified, anthromorphic machine as the hero of stories has, especially in picture books, become a major trend; but it has been carried over to other types of children's literature for various age groups.

[11] Madge Garland, *The Changing Face of Childhood* (London: Hutchinson & Co., 1963), p. 76.

[12] May Hill Arbuthnot, *Children and Books* (Chicago: Scott Foresman & Co., 1947), pp. 303–9.

[13] Cornelia Meigs et al. (eds.), *A Critical History of Children's Literature* (New York: Macmillan Co., 1953), pp. 473–78.

[14] Lewis Carroll, *Through the Looking Glass* (New York: Macmillan Co., 1943), p. 211.

Children's literature is one of the means by which children are socialized and are acquainted with important aspects and features of their civilizations. It is, therefore, only natural that gadgets and machines should loom prominently in children's books in an era and a society that is, in fact, based on technological development. Some of the essential attributes of machinery—its colorfulness, its acoustic quality, and its usually locomotive character—make it especially attractive to children. The many stories and poems in which inanimate machinery plays an important role have the additional task of catering to the child's daydreams and serve the goal of wish fulfilment in fantasy: While the child who dreams of operating machines cannot yet do so in reality, he can do so in fantasy. At the same time, machinery in stories, as in his play, aids him in overcoming fears of the powerful contraption that he harbors in his mind. A good example is the story about "Johnny's Machines,"[15] where the little boy tells his grandfather that he likes to push buttons; so grandfather brings in more and more machines, and the farm becomes mechanized, while Johnny and grandfather are continually proud of and fascinated by the mysterious things. "It was all because Johnny likes to push buttons." Another example would be "Smoky and the Red Fire Engine."[16] A stray dog who is fascinated by the red fire engine one day succeeds in riding on it to be present at a fire where he saves a girl's doll. By this act he gains a home for

himself. The machine's important role is brought out well, but people and dogs are even more important.

In these stories, machines are presented to the child as interesting and intriguing; yet they are mechanical creations of man's ingenuity and nothing else. Adults or children are the stories' actors and heroes. With the appearance of the anthropomorphic machine in children's literature, however, this is changed decisively. They, the machines, are animated; they usually have names and have the ability to think and, even more so, to relate emotionally to others like themselves and to animals and human beings. They become co-protagonists or sole protagonists of the story. The child is expected—this is what the story proposes to him—to enter into a meaningful emotional fantasy relation to it-him-her, exactly as he would be expected to do in a story about a human being or an animal. In other words, he is asked to identify with the machine-hero's exploits and personality. It is assumed that he will learn from them and that these stories will advantageously influence the development of his personality. The fact that, unlike humans and animals and, in fantasy at least, effigies, dolls, and toys, machines have actually only a strictly functional *raison d'être*—this fact is neglected.

Within the confines of the story that humanizes machines, several more or less distinct types can be recognized. The distinction appears to be created mainly by the two criteria of *the degree of intensity with which personification is carried out,* and *the degree of meaningfulness inherent in the machine as protagonist.* In general, the two criteria can be said to be interdependent variables; the more important the machine

[15] Helen Palmer, "Johnny's Machines," in Ellen L. Buell, *A Treasury of Little Golden Books* (New York: Golden Press, 1960), pp. 80–83.

[16] Joseph DeMers, "Smoky and the Red Fire Engine," in Arthur I. Gates, Miriam B. Huber, and Frank S. Salisbury, *Friends and Fun* (New York: Macmillan Co., 1931), pp. 95–106.

is in the story, the more will it-he-she be endowed with biological and psychological attributes.

Type 1.—There are stories in which machines are portrayed in a mild form of personification as having only slight emotional attributes. The emphasis is on the work done together, but a mutual co-operativeness and respect more or less pervade the story: Men care for machines just as machines care for men. Mike Mulligan and Mary Anne, his steam shovel,[17] both work better when admiring people watch their common effort. In the end, they bask together in the town's esteem. The driver of "the taxi that hurried"[18] is proud of his smart little car: *"We're a speedy pair"* (my italics). The taxi "liked to tear along in a hurry, purring softly." "Tuggy the tugboat" and Captain Larson grow old together and do not easily adjust to change:[19] "We like steam boilers, don't we?"; yet in the end they are "now happier than they have ever been before."

These machines are not yet autonomous, but man's superiority over them is only a slight one; he cannot operate without their aid, and, most important, they are alive. As Arbuthnot says of Mike Mulligan and Mary Anne, who has turned from a steam shovel to a furnace, "Both lived a warm, prosperous, and respected life ever after."[20]

Type 2.—In a somewhat similar category are stories like *Maybelle the Cable Car,*[21] and the German story *Henriette Bimmelbahn.*[22] While the accent is as yet on the machine's performance, the emotional attachment becomes more outspoken, and the machine more central as protagonist. *Maybelle the Cable Car* tells the story of how San Francisco's cable cars were saved by the enthusiasm of the city's inhabitants, from the cable car's point of view. While at the beginning the story relates that "she" has a conductor and a gripman, in the end she, in an autonomous decision, gratefully invites the people for a free ride. The reader is told what she and her sisters think, remember, the moods that grip; the limit between machines and human beings is felt less. Henriette Bimmelbahn is actually a grandmother figure; together with her engineer she chugs on, readily leaves the rails to bring the children to the woods, waits patiently until the last of them has picked all the flowers he wants, together with the engineer is very upset when the train collides with a cow, and returns home tired but still good-natured.

Type 3.—This type is the newest version of the "tale of the young hero," the hero being the machine. In the face of fearfully grim odds and after (relatively) unbelievable adventurous exploits, the hero is victorious, and the spice of the story is provided by the contrast; whoever seemed to be strong and powerful suddenly finds himself dependent on the achievements of one who was until now held to be small, helpless, bashful, and inferior.

In fact, this type is a transmutation, a continuation of the age-old myth of

[17] Virginia L. Burton, *Mike Mulligan and His Steam Shovel* (Boston: Houghton Mifflin Co., 1939).

[18] Lucy S. Mitchell, Irma S. Black, and Jessie Stanton, "The Taxi That Hurried," in Buell, *op. cit.,* pp. 24–26.

[19] Jean H. Berg, *Tuggy the Tugboat* (New York: Wonder Books, Inc., 1958).

[20] Arbuthnot, *op. cit.,* p. 307.

[21] Virginia L. Burton, *Maybelle the Cable Car* (Boston: Houghton Mifflin Co., 1952).

[22] James Krüse and Lisl Stich, *Henriette Bimmelbahn* (Berlin: Der Kinderbuchverlag, 1956).

the "young hero," one of the oldest and most persistent motifs in mythology, legend, literature, and children's literature, whose profound psychological significance has been analyzed, in our time, by many writers.[23] It is intimately connected with the motif of "rebirth through suffering" and has been told from time immemorial as the story of young gods and of mortals, bearing, for the weak and oppressed in every culture and for the small and subdued ones growing up in any generation, the message of eternal hope—that one day the despised will stand out as the savior, restrain the mighty, and administer justice. Moses and Pharaoh, Joseph and his brothers, David and Goliath, Hercules and his tasks, Siegfried and the dragon, Cinderella and her stepmother and stepsisters are variants of this paradigm. During the last decades, with the development of children's literature, this motif has been reworked and retold countless times, of adventurous young children who are held in scorn, of adventurous doggies, kittens, young bears, etc., who defy the authority of their elders and return triumphant, having learned something about themselves and the world. On the way, the motif has often acquired a trivial or picayune mode; yet its unflagging universal popularity testifies to its psychological meaningfulness. Of late, it has become the nucleus of accounts of adventurous and misjudged young machines.

The Little Red Engine, in an Israeli version of a British title,[24] is held in contempt by the big overland streamlined locomotives, for all he does is slowly trudge his way over small distances. Yet the day comes when the superengine bearing the king and his entourage jumps the rails in a snowstorm. The stationmaster is in despair, but Little Red Engine saves the day. After an excited dialogue between the two, the stationmaster entrusts the undersized engine with the king's train. During his long journey, the engine goodnaturedly talks with engines, frogs, and people. After triumphantly entering the capital, he returns home and, acclaimed by all the big, important engines, returns to his former modest life, full of inner happiness.

Young Homer[25] is a shiny red caboose; he is gay, "lively as a newborn colt. . . . Railroad steam is in his blood, and there's adventure in his eye." He loses his home train and makes friends with the animals, the human beings, and the old engine of a circus. When they all are in danger of being derailed and thrown into the deep gorge, Homer, putting his right wheel forward, in concert with the animals and against incredible odds, saves them and himself from certain death. No human intervention is needed. Human beings appear only at the end of the story, when the whole town turns out to acclaim Homer the hero and to cheer the brave animals.

The main characteristics of this type are these: The hero is inferior and weak, and different from the rest; a catastrophical situation of some kind—

[23] Among the most important books that have dealt with the subject, one might mention: Otto Rank, *The Myth of the Birth of the Hero,* trans. F. Robbins and S. E. Jelliffe (New York: Journal of Mental and Nervous Diseases Publ. Co., 1914); Joseph Campbell, *The Hero with a Thousand Faces* (New York: Pantheon Books, 1949); Erich Neumann, *The Origins and History of Consciousness,* trans. F. C. Hull (New York: Harper & Row, 1962).

[24] Rahel Caspi, *Ma'assah Bekattar Kattan Adamdam* (Tel Aviv: El Hama'ayanne Publishers, n.d.).

[25] Hardie Gramatky, *Homer and the Circus Train* (New York: G. P. Putnam's Sons, 1957).

storm, fire, breakdown, and so forth—reveals him as the one and only rescuer, through "staggering task or action and . . . considerable suspense";[26] the task he fulfils is socially significant and connected more or less with his work or function as a machine. The former social stigma is replaced by grateful recognition of his feats. Up to this point, the type follows the general outline of the "young hero" story. It differs from it in two ways: (1) While the traditional young hero becomes, after his return, the leader of his kind, this is not true here: socially he becomes equal to them but subsides into his old position. Not achieving a position of leadership is important, but gaining full, social status by proving oneself and so shedding one's role as an outsider is crucial. (This is true also of the modern young child-hero and the animal-hero.) (2) The other dissimilarity results from the peculiar nature of the new hero. He usually maintains cordial relations, based on mutual understanding, with men and occasionally with animals. They all live in "one world."

Actually, this is a mixed type, considering the extent of autonomy. Some of the machines depend upon the close co-operation of men in their work; others operate in full autonomy, driven (sic) by their own discernment and conscience.

Type 4.—This type contrasts with the story of the young hero by stating unequivocally that adventure does not pay. It is one form of the modern moralizing and cautionary tale.

Two main subtypes can be distinguished. The first presents engines that become involved in adventures because they feel an urge to be free of the restrictions placed upon them by man: that is, they are essentially inferior to and dependent on human beings, and while they are allowed to enjoy the adventure, they learn that work and responsibility are preferable.

In the Russian "The Story of a Holiday,"[27] the truck for once wanted to have a good rest on his day off. He felt hot under his roof and left. The green traffic light winked, saying, "Where is your driver?" The automobile understands the problem: "I cannot run alone, and still I do run alone; so what? It's a day off today, and it would be a sin not to go for a trip." Reflecting further on his own strange situation, he finds that "they probably decided to direct me by radio. So what, after all this is the twentieth century, the century of miracles. Let's go on!" The truck pulls off the road and into the woods. After a good rest, his responsibility exerts itself again, and wandering lonely between oaks and birches, he collects a full load of mushrooms which he carries back to his garage. "And now he runs more gladly and carries his loads better."

Choo-Choo,[28] by Virginia Burton, is the story of a little engine who ran away. Normally the little engine had an engineer, a fireman, and a conductor; she pulled cars full of people, and a baggage car; she did her job well. One day, however, she was tired and said to herself, "I could go farther and easier by myself—people would say, 'what a smart little engine.' " She escapes, goes wild, jumps over an open

---

[26] Arbuthnot, op. cit., p. 307.

[27] V. Berestov, "Shaska pro Vuikhodnoi djen," Karzinki v Lushakh (Moscow: Ministerstya Kultur, 1962).

[28] Virginia L. Burton, Choo-Choo: The Story of the Little Engine Who Ran Away (Boston: Houghton Mifflin Co., 1937).

drawbridge, rushes through the big railway yard, and loses her way. When she is rescued by the combined efforts of many people, she is very glad to be found and tells Jim, the engineer, that she will not run away again.

While this story belongs to the first subtype, in which the adventures are usually described as delightful and where the machine is normally operated by human beings, the accent put on the cautionary elements in Choo-Choo's adventure is more reminiscent of the second subtype. Here the cautionary and moralizing intention becomes stronger and more outspoken. Another change is that the human operator disappears and the engine acts on his or her own.

The *Little Freighter*[29] is socially a lower-class boat; other boats deride her: She is so squat, so deep in the water. When she is unloaded, she dances lightly on the water and feels better, is more like the others. But she gets frightened in a storm—"Oh dear, what is happening to me?"—is again derided by her fellow boats, and wishes to be loaded again and to be deep and safe in the water; and then the other boats will not be jealous. Adventure teaches that it is best to keep one's social station and acquiesce in it.

Tootle[30] is an outstanding example of the close mutual relations and understanding among men, machines, and animals. Tootle is a young locomotive who goes to engine school. His fellow students are engines, his teachers men. The two main lessons taught in the school are "Stop at the red light" and

"Stay on the rails no matter what." The reward for being a good student is to become a big streamliner. Tootle is one of the best students the school has had in a long time. Yet one day he finds out how delightful it is to leave the tracks and to look for flowers, so "The Dreadful Thing" happens, and Tootle becomes quite giddy with all the sunshine, the flowers, and the frogs. He is seduced by a black horse and races it across the fields. Tootle's human teachers are consternated. Tootle's fellow (engine) students look down upon him. The school principal informs the mayor, who in turn alerts the citizens, and all combine to return Tootle to the track. By holding up red flags wherever he turns in his escapades among the flowers, they bewilder him; then he discovers his teacher, who stands on the track signaling him with the green flag. The young engine who grew enthusiastic about flowers and fell in love with a horse is chastised by men's care and solicitude. By foregoing his individualistic leanings and conforming to the signals, he will earn 100 A+.

The notable characteristics of this type of story are, then, rather narrowly moralistic. The spirit of adventure leads to errors of judgment and to disaster. As one's elders know better, one should listen to them and prove oneself by hard work, keeping to one's station in life.

Type 5.—The Brave Bookmobile[31] represents yet another type of story characteristic of our times. Every morning the bookmobile sets out to do its work, modestly and usefully, like any anonymous worker. This is a variant of one of the possibly less fortuitous inventions of Progressive Education: the realistic, and didactic, and dull story

[29] Clara Lambart, "Little Freighter," in L. S. Mitchell and I. S. Black (eds.), *Believe and Make Believe* (New York: E. P. Dutton & Co., 1956), pp. 166-70.

[30] Gertrude Crampton, *Tootle* (New York: Simon & Schuster, 1946).

[31] Grover Page, *The Brave Bookmobile* (Indianapolis: E. C. Seale & Co., 1966).

that tells about the unknown everyday hero whose dedication and perseverance make possible the smooth workings of society and safeguard our lives.

Though most stories can be assigned to one of these types, there are exceptions, of course. One rather absurd example is *Ivor the Engine*,[32] an English book whose story is set in Wales. Ivor lived in a shed, did its work conscientiously, in harmony with its human operators. One day, however, Ivor hears the Choral Society practicing. From that moment he is not his own old self any more. "And that night he went to bed very, very sad." Soon the humans notice; he is examined, and "mechanically speaking, I've never seen a better one. It's my belief he's upset. You haven't spoken to him harshly, have you?" In the end, the human operators find out what is wrong because a tear drops from Ivor's window. Organ pipes are fitted to him, the Choral Society looks forward to his participation, and the railway company agrees to it. Before the rehearsal starts, "Ivor suddenly felt funny in his boiler, oh dear, quite queasy. Nervous he was." But then he "was so pleased that he quite forgot to feel nervous." When the story ends, the Choral Society stands and sings, and Ivor, on the railway tracks—*ad maiorem machini gloriam*—as in olden times people gathered near to the organ, only the organ did not weep, and people did not sing to help it. But now, similar to what happened in *Tootle*, Ivor's psychomechano-therapy is carried out, as the dust jacket says, "with the help of nearly everybody else in that part of Wales."

These books constitute, of course, only a small sample of the existing literature in many countries. A list of literature for children and adults referring to engines and prepared toward an exhibition arranged for the International Youth Library (in Munich in 1955) by H. Künnemann, contains some two hundred items in six languages, many of them stories about personified machines. This list also reflects the fact that these books are to be found in translations to many languages.

The anthropomorphic machine has gained importance mainly in picture books for children aged three to seven. But it has not stopped there. In the last few years it has also appeared—influenced by recent scientific developments—in the literature written for older children, especially in the form of stories about androidal robots.

This type of literature has an interesting early forerunner, *The Wizard of Oz*.[33] Two man-made creatures, very different from each other, appear in the story. One is the Scarecrow, who feels like a new man when Dorothy, the heroine, sets him on the ground. He adds, however, " 'I don't know anything. You see, I am stuffed, so I have no brain at all,' he answered sadly." This last word proves that he has emotions at least. As the story develops he demonstrates no little helpfulness, and he has the great advantage of never being tired. The other man-made figure is the Tin Woodman. When Dorothy finds him, he is tin-made throughout, and the only thing she can do for him is to take an oil can and oil his rusty joints. Yet he once was a perfect human being who lost his biological body, part by part, because of his stubborn love for a girl that was opposed by some wicked woman. Limb after limb was replaced with a tin one made by a tinsmith. Now he has no heart and so does not care. Yet he feels

---

[32] Oliver Postgate, *Ivor the Engine* (London: Abelard-Schuman, 1962).

[33] Frank L. Baum, *The Wizard of Oz* (Indianapolis: Bobbs-Merrill Co., 1920).

that something is missing. This modern fantasy is halfway between Andersen and the sixties of the twentieth century: The animation of the inanimate is possible because the setting is a magic country, and a magically endowed girl performs it in harmony with the age-old tradition; on the other hand, the problem of how far man is superior to his creations, and of humanization-dehumanization has a definitely modern ring. The Scarecrow and the Tin Woodman are man-made contraptions that are able to create emotional appeal in humans.

Children's books about robots written in the 1960's, inspired by adult science fiction, treat robots as equal to humans. *Andy Buckram's Tin Men*[34] is an adventure story for boys. Its hero is a boy who builds robots out of tin cans. In the beginning, they are ordinary robots fit for just one very simple job, or less than that; they are operated by being plugged in. At a certain moment in the story, however, lightning that strikes them causes a transformation: while they still have no minds, in their new state of electrification they are able to understand human language. From then on—and actually even before this point—human beings relate to the robots, have feelings for them, attempt to make them feel joyful just as they feel joy at their rescue. The three children, a boy and two girls, one a baby, intermingle with the four robots, one "girl" and three "boys," one a baby, and rely on them for their safe return from danger, while the role of the mastermind remains securely with Andy.

The most curious element in this story is the development of Campbell, the first and youngest of the robots. As things evolve it becomes clear that

Campbell is a mutation of the traditional despised young hero. Campbell arouses emotions from the first. For about two-thirds of the story he is liked by all the female figures in the book and held in scorn by his creator; and Campbell himself, too, develops the power of emotion. He sits down shyly by himself with his head hanging. Then he accepts Sparrow's (Andy's girl friend's) handkerchief and presses it against his cheek. He grows up a little, and later, he saves the human baby from the big bear, and Andy recants and recognizes the real hero in him. At the same time, Campbell has somehow matured.

The story ends in a strange way. Because of a wrong command given by Andy, the robots row away, and they and the boat are lost. Andy and Sparrow very speedily console themselves for the loss by prying out of the sand a new tin can, the start of a new batch of robots. The ending is curious, too. The robots row away, independently, into an unknown future and are immediately forgotten by their human friends. This throws a strange light on the emotional attachments that evolved all through the almost two hundred pages of the story. There is a certain inconclusiveness in this ending concerning the relations between men and their machines.

The Runaway Robot[35] is the story of a robot's indelible friendship with the son of his owners, as told by Rex the robot himself. His personality is very rich in its emotional possibilities: Rex learns to worry, to care, to act independently, being motivated by love, and even to be happy. Yet more: he becomes involved in moral questions. A police sergeant informs him, "You'll have to learn that about humans, Rex. . . . They say a lot of irresponsible

(New York: Viking Press, 1966).

[34] Carol R. Brink, *Andy Buckram's Tin Men*

[35] Lester Del Rey, *The Runaway Robot* (Philadelphia: Westminster Press, 1965).

things. They aren't as reliable as robots."

While in the story the question of superiority of human or robot is not solved, it is clear that its hero is the robot, not the boy.

It should be emphasized that not a few of the stories mentioned here are fun to read and have a humor and charm of their own. Others are trite and trivial. This is true of this as of any other type of story.

These, then, are some of the animated artifacts and machines that serve as protagonists. The child reader is supposed to identify with them; he is asked to learn from them and to emulate them; he is induced to relate to them, and it is assumed that in his fantasy he will look upon them as communicating with him.

It appears that this kind of children's literature has not brought into being any new types or motifs. It has, however, created a new and questionable type of hero; by extending the limits of animism, modern fantasy has originated the story in which animated and personified objects and machines are equal to and often superior to the human beings with whom they live together in "one world."

FANTASIES FOR ADULTS

Children's literature is not, and never has been, an isolated phenomenon. Very early in the evolution of modern technology, the overt attitude of admiration and pride, and the usually covert one of uneasiness and fear, created an unconscious conflict about machines in the mind of Western man. As so often in the individual and collective history of man, when he is confronted with a conflicting mental attitude toward forces beyond his control, he turns, in his attempt to solve the conflict, to the device

of projecting onto these forces the human attributes of emotion, reason, and volition, by way of animation and personification. In this manner the modern anthropomorphic myth of the machine is born; from the outset the myth has these two often intermingling aspects: (1) the *Promethean*—the machine as a powerful servant "who" aids man to subordinate nature; and (2) the *apocalyptic*—the fear of man's losing mastery over what he has created. Later a third aspect of the myth will come into existence: the machine as *a benevolent and equal companion* to man; resulting from the effort to bring it-him-her "into the family."

Since the first half of the nineteenth century, literary expression reflecting realistically, metaphorically, and symbolically man's predicament of having to adapt mentally to his inventions has proliferated. In the following comments, an attempt is made to assess the place of children's literature on animistic machines within the framework of adult culture as a whole.

As a necessary correlate of this development, a new issue appears—the danger of the dehumanization of man and the mechanization of human relations. This is foreshadowed in the nineteenth century, for example, in the writings of Dickens, Melville, and Henry Adams.

Promethean personification is found relatively little, for whenever man's ingenuity is praised, the machine usually remains inanimate. Thomas Wolfe writes: "One feels the brakes go on when the train is coming to a river, and one knows that old gloved hand of cunning is at the throttle. One's own sense of manhood and mastery is heightened by being on a train."[36]

[36] Thomas Wolfe, *You Can't Go Home Again* (New York: Harper & Bros., 1934), p. 55.

Yet Wolfe, who is ever fascinated by men and machines, does personify machinery, when some anxiety is involved: "They believed in that ship, and suddenly they loved her. They loved her delicate, bending strength, her proud undulance that was like the stride of a proud, beautiful woman."

The *ambivalent vision*, the inner tension that results from conflicting attitudes, can be illustrated in Stephen Vincent Benét's verses:

The great, metallic beast . . .
The genie we have raised to rule the earth,
Obsequious to our will
But servant-master still,
The tireless serf already half a god . . .[37]

A similar mood is expressed in a charming little poem: A tourist from outer space asserts that the creatures of this star are composed of metal and glass; their legs are circular, and they turn round and round; they have four eyes, and the two in the back are red. The question the tourist has not yet found the answer for is: those soft shapes that can be seen, like shadows, inside the transparent body—are they their guts or their brains?[38]

These examples illustrate the motif in our thinking that has been formulated by Bruno Bettelheim: "While our progress can be measured by the fact that the machine is clearly recognized as the servant of man and not his better, the fear is now widespread that it could become our master."[39]

The *apocalyptic personification* is illustrative of Fromm's more pessimistic

formulation: "While creating new and better means for mastering nature [man] has become enmeshed in a network of those means. . . . While becoming the master of nature, he has become the slave of the machine which his own hands built."[40]

Čapek's play, *R.U.R.*,[41] is one of the first full-length treatments of the theme. Man succeeds in creating robots that are similar to man except for their inability as yet to act independently and to have emotions. But later, while among men a movement is under foot to guarantee their civil rights, the millions of robots revolt and overcome and exterminate man. Then the robots develop the ability to experience feelings: they are now afraid of death; and as a robot and a robotess love each other, a new race is born that will inherit the earth. The apocalyptic significance of the play is enhanced by this seemingly optimistic ending: if nothing is gained by the extinction of the human race, at least nothing is lost.

The manifestly apocalyptic approach, according to Moskowitz' Introduction to *The Coming of the Robots*,[42] is typical of early science fiction in the nineteenth century and the first decades of the twentieth.

A variation of this view is the view of the machine, and especially the locomotive, as a symbol of forces, of higher powers, of the dreadful and incomprehensible. Künnemann makes the point that "the number of authors is legion,

[37] Quoted in *Education in a Changing Society* (Washington: National Education Association, 1964), p. 31.

[38] May Swenson, "Southbound on the Freeway," *New Yorker*, **38** (February 2, 1963), 32.

[39] Bruno Bettelheim, *The Informed Heart: Autonomy in a Mass Age* (Glencoe, Ill.: Free Press, 1960), p. 61.

[40] Erich Fromm, *Man for Himself: An Inquiry into the Psychology of Ethics* (New York: Rinehart & Co., 1947), p. 4.

[41] Karel Čapek, *R.U.R.* (*Rossum's Universal Robots*) (New York: Samuel French, 1923).

[42] Sam Moskowitz (ed.), *The Coming of the Robots* (New York: Collier, 1963), pp. 177–203. The story was first published in 1934.

in whose writings the locomotive and the train stand for the Nemesis of the ancients," and cites Tolstoi (*Anna Karenina*), A. Döblin (*Berlin-Alexanderplatz*), F. Durrenmatt (*The Visit of the Old Lady*), A. Schwarz-Bart (*The Last of the Just*), and others.[43]

Psychological research testifies to the significance of these phenomena. In a section entitled "Delusions for Moderns," Bruno Bettelheim writes:

What is so new in the hopes and fears of the machine age is that savior and destroyer are no longer clothed in the image of man; no longer are the figures that we imagine can save and destroy us direct projections of our human image. The transition from the useful but mindless machine to the manipulator if not the killer of man is viewed not as a change in kind, but a change in quality or degree.[44]

The term "Delusions for Moderns" reminds one of the fact that, back in 1899, Thorstein Veblen suggested that animism in relation to objects and situations is characteristic of predatory cultures. Not much has happened since then to disprove his hypothesis.[45]

How can it be explained, then, that alongside the Promethean and the apocalyptic, there appears the third view— that of the *humanized and benevolent* machine? Defined more precisely, the machine appears to be a creature similar to man and to have human attributes. It is man's associate and equal companion; it is, to repeat the formulation used above, brought into the family. In fantasy, it is a living thing, not really different from man.

This strange conception has become a mainstay of modern fantasy. To be sure, to some extent it must have existed before our time, but now it has become a major motif.

At the end of the nineteenth century J. K. Huysmans, in his novel *À Rebours,* has the central character fall in love with "two locomotives recently put into service."

One of these, bearing the name of Crampton, is an adorable blonde with a shrill voice, a long slender body imprisoned in a shining brass corset, and supple cat-like movements; a smart golden blonde whose extraordinary grace can be quite terrifying when she stiffens her muscles of steel [and] sends the sweat pouring down her flanks. . . . The other, Engerth by name, is a strapping saturnine brunette, given to raucous guttural cries.[46]

The theme is also ubiquitously treated in satire: In "Ever-Lovin' Machine,"[47] a deceived human lover tells of the mechanical girl he built and loved until she ran off with the toaster.

If machines can love and be loved, they can relate and be related to in other ways as well. In "I, Robot,"[48] the machine, significantly named Adam Link, is possessed by feelings of loyalty and friendliness for humans and becomes a monster only because of their lack of comprehension.

If so, machines can also be viewed as children. Cartoons illustrate this: Scientist to robot: ". . . and stop calling me Daddy."[49]

Similarly, machines can hold a position of authority: Cartoon: Receptionist to client: "Our computer will see you now, sir."

They may exhibit typical human

---

[43] Horst Künnemann, "Musen und Maschinen" (unpublished lecture, Munich, International Youth Library, Summer, 1955), pp. 10–11.

[44] Bettelheim, *op. cit.*, pp. 52–54.

[45] See Thorstein Veblen, *The Theory of the Leisure Class* (New York: Modern Library, 1931), p. 279.

[46] Quoted in Eric Rhode, "The Artist as Seducer," *Listener* (London), May 2, 1936, p. 754.

[47] Shel Silverstein, "Ever-Lovin' Machine," *Playboy,* 12 (December, 1965), 148.

[48] Eando Binder, "I, Robot," in Moskowitz, *op. cit.*, pp. 25–45. The story was first published in 1938.

[49] *Ha'aretz* (Tel Aviv), March 24, 1965, p. 9.

frailties: Cartoon: Two scientists in front of a computer: "It has a tendency to daydream."[50] Cartoon: Two scientists in front of computer, reading tape: "I'll be damned. It says, 'Cogito, ergo sum.' "[51]

What then—to repeat the question—are the sources of this creation of fantasy, the machine experienced as intimately close, understandable and understanding?

The Promethean view is an uncomplicated, conscious expression of justified pride in man's ingenuity: it represents an optimistic acceptance of his achievements and, implicitly or explicitly, hopeful expectations for the future for increasing his mastery. The apocalyptic view expresses man's profound apprehension and anxiety when confronted with seemingly unruly forces that compel him to undergo rapid and extensive changes and yet to cling fearfully to horizons lost forever. Man resorts to animation and personification of the inanimate—as individual and collective man has tended to in his development whenever his mind was faced with the incomprehensible. Is the humanized-benevolent-equal view, then, a symbolic revelation of legitimate affection, of acquiescence to a phenomenon that has come to stay? Some would have it like this.

Animation and personification of the inanimate is, however, not a rational process—it is not the recognition of something that exists objectively. It is a symptom of irrational, and largely un-

conscious, processes; it is a projection of human characteristics onto objects that in fact cannot actually possess them. When this is done consistently, over a long period, it reveals the problematic importance of this category of objects.[52]

The personification of the machine as humane is, in this conception, nothing but the result of a repressive tendency, a transformation, a masking, of the apocalyptic one, in the face of mounting anxiety. This can be gauged by the fact that, when examined more closely, not a few of the "equal" machines brought in above as examples of the benevolent view turn out to be subtly superior.

Modern animism in general, then, is an expression of unrest and ambivalence in Western culture; the resulting conflict is represented in imagery that is symptomatic of man's concern with his place in society and with his human essence.

Specifically, animation and personification that portray the inanimate object as benevolent and intimately responsive, as existing on the same level of life as man, symbolize the intensification of anxiety to an unbearable degree. The conflict is ousted from consciousness by the projection of human, attractive, and pleasing attributes onto the objects. Thus the conflict is hidden or at least disguised. The machine that has a

---

[50] In a collection of cartoons called "A Study of the Unique Influence of Space-Automation Technology in the Present Day Environment, with Special Attention to Its Implications for the Behavioral Sciences: A Symposium of Enlightened Opinion," compiled by Audio Devices, Inc. (n.d., n.p.).

[51] *Ibid.*

[52] "The conscious knowledge of the nature of a mechanical device can . . . coexist with a non-rational magic conception of the instrument. The two views are on different psychical levels and could contradict each other only if both were conscious. . . . Where such a contrast is consciously felt as a contradiction, neurotic patients often regress to an animistic belief that inorganic objects too have a will and a soul" (Theodor Reik, *Listening with the Third Ear* [New York: Farrar, Strauss & Co., 1948], p. 114).

soul is not dangerous any more; it is reasonable.[53]

The process of projection has a reverse side, as it were, an almost natural correlate: The sense of inferiority engendered by the machine seeks relief through one more defense mechanism, the process of identification.

The functioning of this unconscious mechanism, together with the ubiquitousness of machines in modern life, makes it understandable why, supplementing the attribution of human characteristics to machines, modern fantasy offers so many instances of conferring machinelike traits upon human beings. This feature is typical for a technological civilization that struggles for its maturity. It could be documented by examples to be found on all levels of the creative arts.

Andrei Voznesensky, the poet, writes: "That redhead, like someone bespattered with egg yolk, is transformed into a pneumatic drill."[54]

Or, one teenage student in a class I taught, in discussing a poem narrating King Saul's last moments in his battle against the Philistines, summed up her impression by saying that "he was moving about like an excited teleprinter."

But there is more to this. In much of the creative expression of our time, in art and in science, there can be found a strange, growing awareness of man and machine living in "one world" and drawing nearer to the point of becoming, in a sense, mutually interchangeable.

Actually, even this began in the nineteenth century. McLuhan makes the point that

As early as 1872, Samuel Butler's Erewhon explored the curious ways in which machines were coming to resemble organisms not only in the way they obtained power by digestion of fuel but in their capacity to evolve ever new types of themselves with the help of the machine tenders. This organic character of the machines, he saw, was more than matched by the speed with which people who minded them were taking on the rigidity of and thoughtless behaviorism of the machine.[55]

One day, probably, Walt Disney's animated cartoons will be recognized as a major symbol of this process of mutual interchangeability: are those jerky creatures not both mechanical men and hominoid mechanisms? In fact, Marcel Duchamp made the same point much earlier in his painting, "Nude Descending Staircase, No. 2."

Behind this, of course, lurks the spectre of dehumanization. How serious is all this? Serious enough to call for the attention of the scientist and the philosopher: Scientist Norbert Wiener, the man who created cybernetics, warns:

I should like to mention a certain attitude of the man in the street toward cybernetics and automatization. This attitude needs a critical discussion, and in my opinion it should be rejected in its entirety. This is the assumption that machines cannot possess any degree of originality . . . that nothing can come out of the machine which has not been put into it. This is often interpreted as asserting that a machine which man has made must remain continually subject to man. . . . On the basis of such an attitude, many people have poohpoohed the dangers of machine techniques, and they have flatly contradicted the early predictions of Samuel Butler that the machine might take over the control of mankind. . . .

It is my thesis that machines can and do

---

[53] This is, of course, a double illusion, the second aspect of which is to assume that human beings, because they have a soul, are reasonable by that token.

[54] Andrei Voznesensky, "Striptease," trans. William Jay Smith, *Life*, 60 (April 1, 1966), 72.

[55] Herbert Marshall McLuhan, *The Mechanical Bride: Folklore of Industrial Man* (New York: Vanguard Press, 1951), p. 99.

transcend some of the limitations of their de-
signers, and that in doing so they may be both
effective and dangerous. . . .

The "Sorcerer's Apprentice" is only one of
many tales based on the assumption that the
agencies of magic are literal-minded. There is
the story of the genie and the fisherman in the
Arabian Nights, in which the fisherman breaks
the seal of Solomon which has imprisoned the
genie and finds the genie vowed to his own
destruction.[56]

Philosopher Hubert Dreyfus of Massachusetts Institute of Technology is
wondering: "If something that we knew
was just a machine could behave intelligently, it would tend to suggest that
maybe we are just machines." Would
such computers have to be considered
conscious beings? Would they raise a
civil liberties problem?[57] And Professor
Mortimer J. Adler asks:

How does man differ from everything else on
earth—from plants and animals, and from
machines, including computers and electric
brains? . . .

If, on the one hand, it can be decisively established that man does not differ radically
from other animals and machines, what difference will this make to traditional religious beliefs about man's special dignity and destiny,
and to the juridical, political, and moral principles that rest on the distinction between
man and thing?[58]

It appears, then, that the anthropomorphic machine in children's literature
is not an isolated phenomenon. It is one
facet of a growing myth.

[56] Norbert Wiener, "Some Moral and Technical
Consequences of Automation," *Science,* 131 (May
6, 1960), 1355–58.

[57] "What (If Anything) to Expect from Today's
Philosophers," *Time,* 87 (January 7, 1966), 25.

[58] Mortimer J. Adler, "Six Lectures on the Difference of Man and the Difference It Makes"
(Encyclopaedia Britannica Lectures, University
of Chicago, 1966).

THE ANTHROPOMORPHIC MACHINE AS
AN EDUCATIONAL EXPERIENCE

Machine animation can, in fantasy
for the adult, assume three forms: the
Promethean, the apocalyptic, and the
benevolent. In children's literature,
however, only benevolent animation appears. If the hypothesis offered above is
correct, and benevolent animation is the
result of anxiety repressed and forced
into the unconscious, to reappear in the
form of human characteristics projected
onto the machine, then stories about
animated objects written by adult writers for children are a medium through
which adults unconsciously communicate to children their own repressed
anxieties. If this is so, then this type of
literature unwittingly prepares the child
for acquiescence to a "one-world" situation,[59] for life in a society whose
members experience an unconscious inferiority vis-à-vis machines and make
an effort to adapt to them. Then engines can teach the rules of life, that is,
they assume superego functions. "Machines are looking at you"—Andersen's
paranoid streak has become socialized.

As unconscious anxiety is clearly a
psychological hindrance to the development of a healthy personality and to
mature (as against dehumanized) ad-
justment to life, children's literature of
this kind cannot be viewed favorably
from the educational point of view.

Another issue is the danger of func-
tionalization of human relations in a
machine age. The machine hero and its
story can be easily recognized as a particularly apt medium through which to
reinforce these tendencies: The machine's pride lies first and foremost in

[59] In the sense in which this term has been used
in the present paper: humans, animals, and machines living together.

its functional perfection, in its flawless performance; it is satisfied with a relative paucity of relationships. The machine actually has no individuality—one caboose and one railway engine have almost exactly the same makeup and the same problems as the rest of them; it has the typically trivial personality that is representative of—and unwittingly aids to prepare children for—the functional co-operative anonymity required by industrial society. In addition, machines almost never are allowed to play; they usually work and work and are quite happy with it. They are represented as children, but they do not live a child's life. They are happier and more adjusted when they do some useful work. They are reliable because they have learned that the spirit of adventure and of playfulness leads to disaster. They are representatives of a very narrow functionalistic technical ethos.

One more point may be mentioned: The constant and accumulating betrayal of the child's aesthetic experience by this type of literature is an affront to his taste. He ought to be offended by an illustration showing a machine ogling at butterflies; by the spectacle of one machine expressing his love for another by flowers brought by a human;[60] by a truck collecting mushrooms by itself; by being taught the joys of music by a steam engine; by being shown a steam shovel that lives, happily metamorphosed into a furnace, in a cozy cellar with a human being; by being told by numberless illustrators that their grotesque, smiling, or melancholy engines' headlights see light and motion, like animals, while they really emit light.

Should so much weight be attached to a type of literature that is, after all, only one among many? Again and again one is tempted to put these stories aside and shrug them off.

But then, these stories are read by millions of children. And again, psychological, sociological, educational, and scientific writing makes it clear that they are but one facet of that modern myth which has sprung up in our era, and not a myth alone: The struggle between the dehumanization of man and its alternative, the humanization of industrial society, takes place both in man's fantasy and in his reality, on the psychological as well as on the technological level. Erikson warns psychologists and educators: "Our child-training customs have begun to standardize modern man, so that he may become a reliable mechanism prepared to adjust to the competitive exploitation of the machine world. In fact, certain modern trends in child training seem to represent a magic identification with the machine, analogous to identifications of primitive tribes with their principal prey."[61]

A few of the machine books will not hurt the child. Many will. And they are unrewarding reading matter. There are still so many stories written that offer the child more wholesome objects for identification.

What the child needs are books that are conducive to the maturing of his own humanness.

What the child needs to be taught by his books—and by his educators—is respect for life and for meaningful relationships with living human beings, of whom he is one.

[60] Don and Lydia Freeman, *Chuggy and Blue Caboose* (New York: Viking Press, 1951).

[61] Erik H. Erikson, "Ego Development and Historical Change," *Identity and the Life Cycle* (New York: International Universities Press, 1959).

WRITING ABOUT SCIENCE FOR CHILDREN

MILLICENT E. SELSAM

To WRITE about science for children an author needs to know science, to know children, and to know how to write—particularly to understand how to communicate with children on their level.

It is natural for children to be curious and to ask questions. This is also characteristic of most scientists at work. They might be said to have maintained a child's curiosity about the world in which they live, and their mode of working is to ask questions, even as children do. The form of questions asked by younger children is most often that of identity-seeking. Children pick up a caterpillar, a beetle, a shell, or the eggs of some sea animal and want to know the name of it. Having found out the name, they lose interest and usually soon forget the name. I have learned through the years not to tell them the name. Now I never know what the object is, no matter how familiar. I say "let's find out" and look it up with them in a simple guide, hoping to encourage the habit of looking up such things for themselves. As a help to remembering the name, I try to encourage them to do something with the object found. If children's interests are to be maintained and encouraged to develop it should be possible to incorporate these techniques into the writing of books.

It was in this way that I was induced to write a book called *Terry and the Caterpillars*.[1] I had known all my adult life that caterpillars spin cocoons but I had never seen them actually do it. Opposite me on the island lived a little girl who kept bringing me caterpillars. We put some huge ones in jars with some

twigs and leaves of the plants on which they were found. The following week both of us saw, for the first time in our lives, the spinning of the cocoon. I saw the effect of this simple scientific observation on the child, felt the excitement myself, and realized that here science met child in a way that could produce a good book.

But how does the writer communicate the excitement of the discovery? It is not enough to say, "Here is an exciting thing. See the way a caterpillar spins a cocoon." The role of the writer is to write the book so that a child can feel he is *participating* in an observation or a discovery. It should send him out looking for his own caterpillars immediately.

A good science book is not just a collection of facts. The biology text *Life*, by George Gaylord Simpson and collaborators, asks, "Are you being a scientist when you count the sand grains on Coney Island beach? No. It is true you are gathering facts, perhaps carefully, but you are probably crazy."[2]

Scientists gather facts that are relative to some theory to be tested or extended. They have well-formed ideas of what is worth studying at any given time. All scientific work is thus approached with an hypothesis in mind. The very essence of science is the search for general rules, which when found, are summarized in laws and theories. In biology we can think of generalizations such as the cell doctrine, gene theory, the theory of evolution. For example, Darwin's concept of evo-

[1] Millicent Selsam, *Terry and the Caterpillars* (New York: Harper & Row, 1962).

[2] George Gaylord Simpson, Colin S. Pittendrigh, and Lewis H. Tiffany, *Life: An Introduction to Biology* (New York: Harcourt, Brace & World, 1957), p. 22.

lution gave us an understanding of fossils, the geologic history of rocks, comparative anatomy, embryology, and the adaptations of animals to their environment. This one concept, by linking many facts, helped to integrate the field of biology.

The purpose of science books should not be to fill a child's head with facts but to give him some idea of the great advances in science made by the linking of many observable facts into fundamental concepts.

A good science book leads to an appreciation of the methods of science. Scientists find the answers to their questions by observing and experimenting. Children are excellent observers, and if they are given a chance to look at things themselves, they will begin to appreciate the kind of patience and effort that goes into careful observation. Science books should encourage this habit of careful observation. A good book on the seashore should move the reader to go out and examine for himself the wonderful life at the edge of the sea. A good astronomy book should turn the reader's eye to the sky and make him want to buy a small telescope. A good nature book should stimulate a young person to hear, see, smell, and taste things—to use all of his senses to observe.

Observation of natural facts should lead to an interest in discovering the cause of the processes and activities observed. Questions of this kind can best be answered by experiment. The late George Sarton, the famous historian of science, had this to say about developing an appreciation of the scientific method in young people:

One may begin [science training] with the purely descriptive parts which require only some power of observation and memory. Thus a good deal of astronomy, geology, anatomy, botany, and zoology, etc. can be explained in a very simple way. The fundamental methods of science can be illustrated by means of easy experiments, and thus will the spirit of experimental philosophy gradually inform the minds of the pupils. It is, of course, this that matters above all. It is perfectly possible—and it is not even difficult—to inculcate the scientific spirit . . . upon children in various proportions according to the age and intelligence of each. . . . No attempt should be made to teach too many facts; there is no point in that. One fact well understood, if possible by means of personal experiments, is more than a hundred learned by rote.[3]

Good science books should certainly avoid incorrect concepts such as teleology, which explains everything in nature in terms of purpose. Statements likes "birds suddenly leave one locality and fly hundreds of miles to another place *so that* they will have food and a warmer climate in the new location" seem to close off all further inquiry. A great deal of serious scientific study is being devoted to the migration of birds. Experiments have led to theories about the length of day influencing the reproductive organs—and to theories about how the whole process may have originated far back in the sequence of ice-age times when birds were forced to move further south. A scientific presentation of migration gives the facts as known to date from observation and experimentation, gives the best theories available, and shows what areas are still to be explored. It avoids the easy and incorrect use of words like "so that," "nature wants or prefers," etc.

Lucretius, the great Roman poet of science of the first century B.C., in his epic poem "On the Nature of Things" had this to say on the subject of teleology almost two thousand years ago.

[3] George Sarton, *The History of Science and the New Humanism* (Cambridge, Mass.: Harvard University Press, 1937), pp. 129–30.

... Avoid I beg you, teleology
With all my heart I long that you should shun
   this fault of reasoning.
Through prudent fear and foresight in advance
This blunder miss:
Don't ever think that eyes were made
In order that the human race might have the
   power to see.

. . . .

Ideas like these which men proclaim are false
   in reasoning,
Abysmally confound effect with cause.
Nothing at all was brought to be in all our
   human frame
In order that the human race might use it.
What is brought to be creates its use.
Vision existed not at all
Before the light of eyes was brought to be.[4]

Another common and equally incorrect concept is anthropomorphism,
which sees everything in nature from a
human point of view. In an article entitled "The Evolution of Mind" in the
June, 1957, issue of *Scientific American*,
Norman L. Munn tells an ancient Chi-
nese story which illustrates the naïve
human attitude in this matter. "Chuang
Tzu and Hui Tzu were standing on the
bridge across the Hao River. Chuang
Tzu said, 'Look how the minnows are
shooting to and fro! How joyful they
are!' 'You are not a fish,' said Hui Tzu,
'How can you know that the fishes are
joyful?' 'You are not I,' answered
Chuang Tzu, 'How can you know I do
not know about the joy of the fishes?
... I know it from my own joy of the
water.' "[5]

Mr. Munn then points out that modern psychology does its best to stop
this kind of anthropomorphic approach
and tries to find out how the animal's
mind works by studying its behavior.

The study of animal behavior is fascinating enough when it is based on the
results of observation and experiment
in the field and is not beclouded with
an approach that ascribes human characteristics to animals.

The question of accuracy with regard to matters of fact in a science book
is actually of much less importance than
the goals above discussed. On this subject, I want to quote from an article by
Eva L. Gordon of Cornell University
entitled "Reviewing and Selecting Nature Books for Children." She says:

Accuracy . . . is not simply a matter of
correct factual detail. . . . Accuracy seems a
much more complex matter than avoidance of
vagueness or misstatement. It implies, for one
thing, discrimination between proved or demon-
strable truth, and hypothesis. An explanation
of the origin of the universe or a description
of the habits and appearance of prehistoric
animals may be stated not as what we believe
to be possible on the basis of evidence we have,
but in terms as positive as might be used to
tell how one made his garden or to describe
the appearance and behavior of a pet cat.
Accuracy means also, a willingness to say, "I
don't know," and in general, avoidance of
sweeping statements and sparing use of such
words as "all," "every," and "always." It
means, too, careful expression in terms not
necessarily technical, but at least not in conflict
with scientific language that will come into
the child's later experience. . . . Good performance in this matter of careful expression,
always practiced by some authors, seems to
be shown increasingly in the newer books,
sometimes in judicious use of scientific names,
and frequently in the use of well-defined, carefully explained terms instead of awkward,
written-down expressions.[6]

Good science books should communicate some of the excitement of discovery—and the triumph that goes with
the solution of scientific problems. They
should make a young person understand
why Archimedes could jump out of his

[4] Lucretius *De rerum naturae* 823–26, 832–36.
Set in English verse by Alban Dewes Winspear
(New York: S. A. Russell, Harbor Press, 1956),
p. 170.

[5] Norman L. Munn, "The Evolution of the
Mind," *Scientific American* (June, 1957), p. 140.

[6] Eva L. Gordon, "Reviewing and Selecting Nature Books for Children," *School Science and
Mathematics*, **49** (November, 1949), 604–5.

bath to rush through the streets of Syracuse shouting "Eureka" when he discovered a new physical principle.

Books about science should help young people to see that our human goals must be shaped by science and that science must be enriched by human hopes and ideals. With man's new control of the forces of nature—with atomic power and earth satellites—science books can help to develop the idea that science is not mere knowledge of things independent of our human purposes or merely a means of giving us material comforts and gadgets but is part of the fabric of our lives. The methods of science can be used to create rational attitudes free of superstition and prejudice.

Two subjects where non-scientific attitudes are readily observable are evolution and sex. Without evolution there is no science of biology, and yet it is impossible to sell a book about evolution for the elementary grades. Dinosaurs are acceptable. There are plenty of books for younger children on this subject, but a careful examination will reveal how few of them make it understood that the age of the dinosaur was a great reptilian upsurge followed by an age in which mammals developed and that this process is part of the evolutionary development of all animals. Even in textbooks for the sixth, seventh, and eighth grade, the word "evolution" will not be found, although various aspects of the subject may be covered. The new revision of the elementary science studies is making a great point of this omission of evolution from the curriculum, and new studies will undoubtedly include it. But it is not now possible to sell a trade book on evolution to libraries in the same numbers that you can sell any other science book—even though it may

have good or better reviews. There seems to be a wall of prejudice on this subject that is not talked about but which nevertheless operates. I can offer as an example a book I wrote entitled *Around the World with Darwin*.[7] This is a simple account of Darwin's *Voyage of the Beagle,* but it has had one-third the sale of my other books.

The same "wall" operates with books on sex—even in animals, let alone humans. I wrote a book called the *Courtship of Animals*,[8] which was well reviewed, and yet this book is selling less than half as many copies as the other books in the same animal-behavior series. By the time a young person is thirteen or fourteen he can walk into any bookstore and buy a paperback explaining sex from *A* to *Z*. But before that time he cannot even learn about courtship and mating in the animal world and see himself in perspective in the world of nature. Squeamishness on the part of parents, teachers, and librarians makes for squeamishness on the part of publishers, and so very few books on evolution and sex are published.

There are many other non-scientific attitudes that abound among us. But these will decline in proportion to the number of good science books read by the new generation. By good science books, to repeat, I mean those that show the methods of science at work, that elucidate basic principles of science and are not a mere assembly of facts, that convey something of the beauty and excitement of science, and that interest young people in thinking up good questions for new young scientists to test by experiment.

[7] New York: Harper & Row, 1961.
[8] New York: William Morrow & Co., 1964.

EVALUATION OF CHILDREN'S RESPONSES TO LITERATURE

DORIS YOUNG

IN ONE of the "Peanuts" cartoon strips, Schulz presented one kind of response to literature as Lucy summarized Snow White. Lucy stalks along as she says: "This Snow White has been having trouble sleeping, see? Well, she goes to this witch who gives her an apple to eat which put her to sleep. Just as she's beginning to sleep real well . . . you know, for the first time in weeks . . . this stupid prince comes along and kisses her and wakes her up."[1] Linus then remarks, "I admire the wonderful way you have of getting the real meaning out of the story." Expressing the "real meaning" is but one response to literature. Response to literature is also evident as it satisfies a child's need. For example, in *Home from Far,* Little describes this response: "Usually when Jenny was sent to her room, she felt it was cheating to read. You forgot all about whatever you had done wrong two minutes after you opened a book. But now she jumped off the bed and went to the bookcase. She wanted a sad book. She was not ashamed of crying over people in a story. She chose *The Birds' Christmas Carol* and curled up in the chair next to the window. Soon she was in another world, where Mother, the two Michaels, and the nightmare of fear she had felt when she had been trapped by the fire could not follow her."[2] Evaluation begins with recognition

that the child's "real meaning" and other responses are internal evaluations. He decides to give attention by evaluating his environment; he evaluates as he selects elements to remember, allows feelings to flow, or permits the alchemy of imagination to work its wonders. However, the concern of this paper is external evaluation. A brief definition of evaluation as a process will be followed by examples of four categories of responses. There is no attempt here to summarize research; the intent is to indicate kinds of investigations that have been made. The analysis will lead to questions that need to be answered.

EVALUATION AS A PROCESS

The first step in the process of evaluation is identification of the kinds of responses that might be observed. Concurrently, it is necessary to make some judgments about the kinds of changes it would be desirable to make as the child spends time in the elementary school. The child does "spend" his time, and educators have no right to insist that he waste this precious coin of life. Thus, the objectives we select are of prime importance. Determining objectives is a part of evaluation. Instead of a synonym for measurement, it is considered to be "a continuous process of inquiry, based upon criteria co-operatively developed in the school-community, which lead to warranted conclusions with respect to how successfully the school is studying, interpreting, and guiding socially desirable changes in

[1] Charles Schulz, "Peanuts," United Features Syndicate, Inc.

[2] Jean Little, *Home from Far,* illus. Jerry Lozare (Boston: Little, Brown & Co., 1965), p. 81.

human behavior."[3] Thus, the design of instruments to gather evidence and the collection and interpretation of evidence about behavior are but parts of a total process. Some educators would urge us not to attempt the measure of responses to literature. They are afraid that the intangible elements, like love, will disappear with analysis. Others fear written tests of cognitive development may overbalance the objective of enjoyment of literature. There is concern that procedures designed for research might become the major teaching strategy. These fears are unjustified if the concept of evaluation of a total situation is kept in mind. Krathwohl and others[4] point out the dangerous "erosion" of educational objectives that are not evaluated. Failure to identify objectives in terms of behavior in both the cognitive and affective domain will only result in further "time-stealing" school activities.

EVIDENCE OF CHILDREN'S RESPONSES TO LITERATURE

Every teacher or librarian is aware of the varied responses of children to literature. Children react differently to the very act of reading or listening. An individual reads for different purposes at different times. Closely related to these interests and attitudes is the category of emotional experience of literature. Meanings and understandings form another category of responses related to a particular selection. A fourth type of response is in the cognitive domain—knowledge of literature as a field. The child's creative products reflect further responses to the experience of literature. All of these responses are components of that elusive term, appreciation.

INTERESTS, ATTITUDES, PREFERENCE

The children respond.—The following expressions reveal some of children's interests and attitudes:

"How many books do you have to read to go to the summer party?"

"Aw, that's a baby book."

"But horse stories are for girls!"

"Nope. I just read science books."

"The author of my book is Elizabeth Speare. The title is *The Bronze Bow*. It's a Newbery book on the list. It has 254 pages. The main character is Daniel. The setting is Galilee. I liked it because it had lots of fights. That's my report."

> I chatter, chatter as I flow,
>   To join the brimming river,
> For men may come and men may go,
>   But I go on forever.

"That's my 100 lines!" (The fourth grader had completed his memorization assignment in the middle of the poem, and sat down with a "clump.")

Investigators' report.—Concerned with the development of citizens who are readers, the school must ask "what does the child do?" as well as "what can he do?" Many studies of reading interests and preferences have been made. For example, Norvell's study of 24,000 children revealed that children do not like what adults think they should or do enjoy.[5] One problem with this study was that there was no investigation of the literature available to the children.

[3] Harold G. Shane and E. T. McSwain, *Evaluation and the Elementary Curriculum* (rev. ed.; New York: Henry Holt & Co., 1958), p. 60.

[4] David R. Krathwohl, Benjamin S. Bloom, and Bertram B. Masia, *Taxonomy of Educational Objectives. The Classification of Educational Goals. Handbook II: Affective Domain* (New York: David McKay Co., 1956), p. 16.

[5] George W. Norvell, *What Boys and Girls Like To Read* (Morristown, N.J.: Silver-Burdett Co., 1958).

Kindergarten children studied by Cappa responded by asking to hear the story again, by looking at the book, or through creative activities.[6] Interests of boys in grades four through six were obtained through interviews by Starchfield.[7] We do have evidence regarding content interests according to age and sex. Interests in poetry have been investigated by Mackintosh in 1932,[8] Kyte in 1947,[9] and recently by Pittmann.[10] In these studies, children selected favorite poems among those read by the teacher. Wells found that adolescents' preferences for humorous literature were influenced by cultural level.[11] In schools having a higher cultural level, satire and whimsy received greater appreciation. Absurdity ranked first, slapstick second, satire third, and whimsy fourth. Gaver developed measures for studying effectiveness of centralized library service.[12] Sixth graders

[6] Dan Cappa, "Kindergarten Children's Responses to Storybooks Read by Teachers," *Journal of Educational Research,* 52 (October, 1958), 75.

[7] Jo M. Starchfield, "Boys' Reading Interests as Revealed through Personal Conferences," *Reading Teacher,* 16 (September, 1962), 41–44.

[8] Helen K. Mackintosh, "A Critical Study of Children's Choices in Poetry," *University of Iowa Studies in Education,* Vol. 7, No. 4 (1932).

[9] George C. Kyte, "Children's Reactions to Fifty Selected Poems," *Elementary School Journal,* 47 (February, 1947), 331–39.

[10] Grace Pittman, "Young Children Enjoy Poetry," *Elementary English,* 43 (January, 1966), 56–59.

[11] Ruth E. Wells, "A Study of Taste in Humorous Literature among Pupils of Junior and Senior High Schools," *Journal of Educational Research,* 28 (October, 1934), 81–91.

[12] Mary Virginia Gaver, *Effectiveness of Centralized Library Service in Elementary Schools (Phase I)* (Report of the research study conducted at Rutgers University under contract no. 489, SAE-8132 with the U.S. Office of Education [New Brunswick, N.J.: Rutgers University, Graduate School of Library Service, 1960]).

maintained complete reading records for nearly four months. Concerned with quality as well as quantity, I developed an instrument to determine levels of maturity in reading.

Further questions.—There have been few, if any, longitudinal studies of reading interests and attitudes. What will be the effect of the libraries made possible by federal funds? What are the opportunities for responding to literature? How do differences in these opportunities affect attitudes and interests? What would be the effect of more co-operative planning of the school librarian and public librarian? What teaching strategies will create a more open response toward varied types of literature? What poems will children select, read to the class, and memorize when given an opportunity to read from many sources?

These are questions to be investigated about groups. Each teacher and each librarian must be concerned with study of the unique patterns of interest of each reader. What records can be maintained easily? What information about reading and listening experiences should become part of the cumulative record? How shall this information guide their work with boys and girls?

EMOTIONAL, IMAGINATIVE RESPONSE

The children respond.—The internal response as the child interacts with visual and auditory symbols may be reflected in overt behavior, or it may be recalled through introspection. Yet, introspection cannot be considered a true account of the process. These responses illustrate behaviors that reflect emotional response:

"Oh!"—on a rising note of surprise as second graders see the picture of Tico's golden wings. Surprise, joy, beauty are surmised.

"Read it again!" after hearing, "Once there was an elephant/who tried to use the telephant/. . ."

"I cried when Biddy died—She was so wonderful . . . And I really liked Peter," says a child after reading *Mountain Born* by Yates. However, it was the unspoken word, the look of mutual understanding that passed between teacher and pupil that reflected the deeper satisfaction.

"I want to read you this poem—not the class, just you," announced the child who wanted to share McCord's "This is My Rock."

"It was awful—just terrible when they were beating the Greyhound," reported a nine year old who reflected some of his horror. Yet he liked the book and commented he felt he had really read a "grown up" book now.

————. This space can only indicate the sudden intake of breath when a nine year old turned a page of *In a Spring Garden* to experience the glowing color of Keats's background for the poem by Issa, "Just simply alive, /Both of us, I/And the poppy/. . ."

"Listen now, I want to tell you about this book, *Island of the Blue Dolphins*. How many have read it? I've read it three times. It's well, sort of a girl's book, but not really. Well, do you *know* about it, what it *really means*?" The fourth grader continued to discuss the plot, characterization, and theme of a book that had deep significance to him.

Evidence of research.—Varied methods have been used to identify and measure emotional response to literature. Hruza used a galvanometer and a pneumograph to note changes as college students listened to fifteen poems.[13] However, introspection indicated some subjects who showed large galvanic reactions were unaware of emotional reaction. This study also showed there was a greater reaction when the subject matter was related to personal experience. Broom also used a galvanometer to determine emotional reactions to specific words.[14] Other investigators

attempted to identify responses through recall of feelings experienced as a selection was heard or read. Valentine asked graduate students to recall the degrees of pleasure, imagery, and details experienced while hearing poetry.[15] He found that imagery or a deliberate attempt to create a visual image may interfere with pleasure. Letton also used the retrospective-verbalization technique in a study of ninth graders' oral reports of their thoughts during reading of poetry.[16] After telling what he thought as he read, the student was asked to look at "thought units" from the poems and tell what he thought about and felt when reading that part of the poem. In 1935, Pooley urged that measures of appreciation be devised and noted that "any measuring instrument which rests exclusively upon the student's ability to identify and explain the sources of appreciation without first measuring his inarticulate sensitivity to them is not a valid test."[17] Indeed it is this "inarticulate sensitivity" that has been neglected. Perhaps the work of Hess in measuring dilation and constriction of the pupil of the eye will give a method for study of inner responses.[18]

The effect of the child's stage of de-

[14] M. E. Broom, "A Study of Literature Appreciation," *Journal of Applied Psychology*, 18 (1954), 357–63.

[15] C. W. Valentine, "The Function of Images in the Appreciation of Poetry," *British Journal of Psychology*, 14 (October, 1923), 164–91.

[16] Mildred C. Letton, "Individual Differences in Interpretive Responses in Reading Poetry at the Ninth Grade Level" (unpublished Ph.D. dissertation, University of Chicago, 1958).

[17] Robert C. Pooley, "Measuring the Appreciation of Literature," *English Journal*, 24 (October, 1935), 631.

[18] Eckhard H. Hess, "Attitude and Pupil Size," *Scientific American*, 212 (April, 1965), 46–65.

[13] Thelma E. Hruza, "An Investigation of Some Factors in the Appreciation of Poetry" (unpublished Ph.D. dissertation, George Peabody College for Teachers, 1940).

velopment has been explored by Peller.[19] She suggested the importance of
literature that supports daydreams for
both boys and girls in the latency stage
and believed that sex differences are of
great importance. Loban's study of
social sensitivity among adolescents
revealed that the reader tended to identify with the character most like himself.[20]

An example of a study of overt responses of two to four year olds as
they listened to stories was made by
Smith.[21] Such behavior as laughter,
smiling, nodding approval, and annoyance behavior was checked.

There are descriptive accounts but
scant research in the area of biblio-
therapy.

Collier and Gaier have published reports of investigations of college students' childhood preferences for literature.[22] Cultural and sex roles are apparently influential factors, and literature may affect acceptance of role. Very
little is known about the relationship
of literature and psychological development. Peller suggested that a child may
have a crucial experience through a

daydream in a story at a time when
he is under stress.[23]

Needed research.—Perhaps our first
concern should be that teachers become
more aware of emotional responses to
literature and provide opportunities for
the child to express his feelings in an
atmosphere of "psychological safety."
We need to know more about the nature
of the experience of literature. What
occurs in the process of "identification"
with a character? What factors lead to
empathy, imagination, identification?
What is the relation of self concept to
imaginative response?

RESPONSES OF UNDERSTANDING
AND INSIGHT

Literal comprehension is not essential
for response to sensory images, rhythm,
or rhyme; perhaps some readers feel
they "stand in the shoes" of a character
without fully comprehending the situation. However, literal comprehension is
the foundation for understanding implied meanings and for perception of
relationships. As children gain insight
into man's relationships with nature,
with other men, and with the super-
natural they gain self-knowledge. There
is a very close relationship of the cognitive and affective responses as values
are internalized and as understanding of
the human condition is applied to life
experience.

Children's responses.—The following
excerpts are from tape recordings of
group and individual discussions of
books. Frequently, we can see the child
fumbling for words to cage fledgling
thoughts: "I just didn't know what it
would be like to be deaf. David was

[19] Lili E. Peller, "Daydreams and Children's
Favorite Books," in J. F. Rosenblith and Wesley
Allinsmith (eds.), *The Causes of Behavior: Read-
ings in Child Development and Educational Psychology* (Boston: Allyn & Bacon, 1962), pp. 405–
11.

[20] Walter Loban, "A Study of Social Sensitivity
(Sympathy) among Adolescents," *Journal of Educational Psychology,* **44** (February, 1953), 102–12.

[21] Lois Z. Smith, "Experimental Investigation
of Young Children's Interest and Expressive Behavior Responses to Single Statement, Verbal Repetition, and Ideational Repetition of Content in
Animal Stories," *Child Development,* **1** (March,
1930), 247–54.

[22] Mary J. Collier and Eugene I. Gaier, "Adult
Reactions to Preferred Childhood Stories," *Child
Development,* **29** (March, 1958), 97–103.

[23] Peller, "Reading and Daydreams in Latency,
Boy-Girl Differences," *Journal of the American
Psychoanalytic Association,* **6** (January, 1958), 57–
70.

lost, and he couldn't even tell anybody." The ten year old had gained insight into problems of a deaf person through reading *David in Silence* by Robinson. "I think Swimmy had to change, you know, he had to swim slower to be the eye. And I think he worried about, well, some little fish might not stay in that place . . . and, uh, it wouldn't be easy." A second grader was perceiving some problems of leadership as he reflected upon *Swimmy* by Lionni. A sixth grader was thinking through the implications of *Harriet the Spy* by Fitzhugh. "No, Harriet wasn't exactly like anybody I know. Who would need a nurse at her age? And in most schools I think you'd have to do your homework instead of writing. But I know about, well, like telling the truth, even if it makes people mad, and . . . some kids are like that, well—before you learn, and it's well, hard to decide." In another discussion, of Holm's *North to Freedom*, the same reader said: "David shouldn't have told the younger children about things being so awful—like you can't trust people . . . and, well, that things are bad. They'll find out, but, like—if I told Laurie about awful things, she'd never go to play, maybe—or she'd be afraid."

Findings from research.—To assess children's understandings of literal and implied meanings we can utilize reading-comprehension tests and vocabulary tests, but there is a need for instruments to measure literary meanings. Garrison and Thomas asked sixth graders to write what they thought a poem was about after hearing it read.[24]

They found a significant relationship between vocabulary ability and discovery of theme, reader participation, and sensory imagery. Weekes presented forty-one poems in original and simplified versions to 412 sixth graders.[25] Figurative language presented more difficulty than "involved sentence structure." She found that actual experience could be a favorable or unfavorable factor in understanding the poem. Foreman held the view that basic appreciation is "a concept of the reality and humanness of the characters in a story; the awareness of story purpose and trend; the pictures which are stimulated by the author's description and completed through the child's experience."[26] The interview method was used to determine meanings seventh graders obtained from excerpts from three prose selections. He developed scales to classify responses to such questions as, "If you were going to paint a picture, what would you put in? Were there any people you would like to know or be with?" In Skelton's study of intermediate-grade children's interpretations of poems, 49 per cent of the responses were denotative interpretations and 35 per cent were meanings "read into" the poem.[27] Most of the children did not go beyond reporting of the details of the four poems read to them.

Tests were developed by Logasa and

[24] K. C. Garrison and M. Thomas, "A Study of Some Literature Appreciation Abilities as They Relate to Certain Vocabulary Abilities," *Journal of Educational Research*, **22** (December, 1930), 396–99.

[25] Blanche E. Weekes, "The Influence of Meaning on Children's Choices of Poetry," *Contributions to Education*, No. 354 (New York: Teachers College, Columbia University, 1929).

[26] Earl R. Foreman, "An Instrument To Evaluate the Literary Appreciation of Adolescence" (unpublished Ph.D. dissertation, University of Illinois, 1951), p. 4.

[27] Glenn Skelton, "A Study of Responses to Selected Poems in the Fourth, Fifth, and Sixth Grades" (unpublished Ph.D. dissertation, University of California, Berkeley, 1963).

McCoy to determine high school students' ability to discover themes in poetry. A test of literary comprehension and appreciation is available for high school students.[28] The studies of critical reading underway at The Ohio State University[29] will provide some instruments that should prove useful.

Further questions.—Most of the investigations have used poetry or excerpts from longer works. We need to study meanings children derive from total works. What selections are appropriate for a measure of literary understandings? When a child returns to a selection in a year or two years, what additional insights will be evident? What is the effect of wide reading upon discovery or understanding of themes? Do particular teaching strategies result in higher levels of insight?

RESPONSES TO LITERATURE AS
A DISCIPLINE

The child's reaction to a specific selection is influenced by his knowledge of literature, authors and illustrators, genre, the craft of writing, and criteria for evaluation. Each discipline does have its mode of inquiry, but in literature there is no one "method of literary study."

Responses of children.—The following examples of children's responses indicate the beginning of awareness that each selection is a part of a larger body of literature: "This is a fantasy," an-

nounced a third-grade reviewer of *The Borrowers Aloft* by Norton. He was implying certain expectations and criteria in recognizing the literary genre. When a large poster copy of the poem, "Brooms," was displayed with the poet's name, second graders expressed interest, "Oh, Dorothy Aldis! We know her poems." Familiarity with the poet established a "set" for the new poem. Upon hearing *Baba Yaga,* by Small, a seven year old said, "It's like Hansel and Gretel—you know, the children in the oven, and the pot in this story." To the question, "What are you reading today?" Lissa replied, "A Nancy Drew— oh, I know it really isn't good writing —but it's fun, and everybody else reads Nancy Drew." Lissa was aware of criteria as we discussed Nancy Drew plots and characterization, but she also wanted to be accepted by her peers. "I know why the South Wind has to be the baker—because a south wind is warm—and he says 'bites' because the north wind bites your fingers." A second grader volunteered this response to Lindsay's, "The Moon's the North Wind's Cooky." "This book isn't as good as *The Loner,*" remarked the ten year old who had just read Wier's new book, *Easy Does It.* His reasons for the statement were supported by evidence. A critic of *The Spider Plant* by Speevack commented, "It just wouldn't be that way. I don't think everybody would come to the play—and they just wouldn't suddenly start being nice." These kinds of responses include what has been called critical reading. The reader separates fact from fiction, draws inferences, recognizes the author's point of view. He evaluates structure of plot, validity of theme, authenticity of setting, depth and real-

---

[28] Mary Willis and H. A. Domincovich, *Cooperative Literary and Appreciation Test* (Princeton, N.J.: Educational Testing Service, 1943).

[29] Charlotte Huck, Martha King, Beatrice Ellinger, and Willavene Wolfe, "The Critical Reading Ability of Elementary School Children" (U.S. Office of Education Project OE 2612 [Columbus, Ohio: The Ohio State University, in progress]).

ism of characterization, use of figurative language. His awareness of the form and arrangement of symbols in creating the total effect is a part of this kind of response to literature.

Evidence from research.—In the thirties there was a surge of interest in testing "appreciation" of literature. To many of the investigators, appreciation was considered recognition of merit. Carroll's high school subjects were asked to rate prose selection,[30] and Speer's sixth graders ranked poetry according to merit.[31] Howells and Johnson devised a test in which high school pupils selected a line of poetry that most nearly fitted the poem.[32] A test designed by Eppel also asked pupils to select the best line of poetry when one was omitted.[33] In Burton's short-story test three possible endings were presented for student selection.[34] The Logasa-McCoy tests attempted to assess ability to identify rhythm and trite and fresh expressions, for example. Very little attention has been given the problem of assessing the elementary school child's knowledge of or awareness of types of literature, sound effects of language, metaphor, plot structure, or characterization.

Huus presented a summary of research related to development of taste in literature in the elementary school.[35] However, many articles cited were descriptive accounts; the majority of the studies were old; there were very few investigations of children in primary grades.

Problems for investigation.—At the present time we do not know what knowledge of literature children possess at the end of elementary school, or at different age levels. What criteria do children use in evaluating the prose and poetry they encounter? What *can* they learn about modes of inquiry? This question should be followed by the question, What *should* they learn about the process of literary criticism in the elementary school? How can a local school system establish guidelines in terms of "standard literary works" children should know, yet provide the flexibility needed for special group and individual needs? An example of a kind of question facing the curriculum-makers is that of biblical literature; if children are to be familiar with the body of literature, with literary allusions, should Bible stories be included in the program? What materials could be used?

How children express awareness of literary style is another kind of question. Before an analysis of teaching materials and methods can be made, it will be necessary to develop instruments to assess such responses. At the

[30] Herbert A. Carroll, "A Method of Measuring Prose Appreciation," *English Journal,* **22** (March, 1933), 184–89.

[31] Robert K. Speer, "Measurement of Appreciation in Poetry, Prose and Art and Studies in Appreciation," *Contributions to Education,* No. 362 (New York: Teachers College, Columbia University, 1929).

[32] Thomas H. Howells and A. A. Johnson, "A Study of Metre-Sense in Poetry," *Journal of Applied Psychology,* **15** (1931), 539–44.

[33] E. M. Eppel, "A New Test of Poetry Discrimination," *British Journal of Educational Psychology,* **20** (June, 1950), 111–16.

[34] Dwight L. Burton, "The Relationship of Literary Appreciation to Certain Measurable Factors," *Journal of Educational Psychology,* **43** (November, 1952), 436–39.

[35] Helen Huus, "Development of Taste in Literature in the Elementary Grades," *Development of Taste in Literature* (Champaign, Ill.: National Council of Teachers of English, 1962).

present time a committee of the National Council of Teachers of English is developing one instrument. Challenged to developed a paper-pencil instrument for grades four to six, the committee has faced the problems of identifying and limiting kinds of responses that could be assessed in this way. We need to know, for example, how responses differ when the selection is read silently by the child and when he hears it read aloud by the teacher. What selections are appropriate for such an instrument? What cues or activities will elicit children's understanding of a selection and their sensitivity to the ways in which the total effect was created by the writer?

RESPONSES TO LITERATURE IN THE CHILD'S CREATIVE WORK

A fourth category of response to literature is the response evidenced in the child's own creative work. The experience of literature becomes part of the child's resources for communicating *his* responses to his environment.

Examples of children's responses.— "Creative work" as viewed in this context does not have to be a tangible product. There is creativity in discussion, for example, when children make comparisons, evaluate, and juxtapose ideas in new relationships. Recordings could be analyzed to identify this type of creativity, but the following examples reflect ways literature may become a catalyst for tangible creative endeavors: "I made a hat like Jennie's," said a first grader as she displayed a creation of her own after hearing Keats's story, *Jennie's Hat*. "Once upon a time in a faraway land . . ." begins a child's story patterned after the folk tales he had heard. "Now you're Robin Hood, and

I'm Little John," the director of backyard dramatic play was overheard to say. "Beyond the fence is Sherwood Forest." "This is a haiku poem I wrote. Can you help me make it sound better in the last line?" requests a sixth grader. In a letter to Taro Yashima, "I think you know just how it is to be a lonely little girl."

Needed research.—To respond to literature with deeper awareness, children need to experience the problems and pleasures of attempting to communicate their experiences. In this paper, we can neither explore nor summarize the research related to creativity. It should be noted that the University of Nebraska curriculum project has been concerned, in part, with the effect of literature upon composition. Further studies of children's writing, painting, and dramatizations are needed to identify responses related to experience with literature.

TEACHERS AND LIBRARIANS AS EVALUATORS

Teachers and librarians have always evaluated children's responses to literature in informal ways. Perhaps they have been satisfied to enjoy the comradely glow when a child finds pleasure in a book they enjoyed. They are happy when they observe good readers seeking and discovering the "realms of gold" in literature. Seldom have there been attempts to discover why some children reach out, why others who can read just as well do not really enter the world of books.

Teachers and librarians do not need to wait for the psychologists and educators to present research. In recent years the concept of "action research" has been neglected, but this approach is needed more than ever before. Librarians and classroom teachers can work together to evaluate the various components of appreciation. They can develop and maintain cumulative records of children's reading interests. They can maintain anecdotal records of the child's use of literary models or allusions to literature in his own writing. Analysis could be made of oral and written book reviews at different times during the year. Records can be made of overt responses as a child reads. Anecdotes could include introspective comments as "I know how it feels," "I have done this." Time can be planned for conferences and small-group discussions so there is opportunity to listen to the child's interpretation of a book. As instruments become available to aid them in gathering evidence about pupil behavior, teachers can use such instruments with wisdom, just as they use intelligence tests, achievement tests, and sociograms to aid in understanding the whole child. The process of evaluation of children's responses to literature must gain priority among the present professional tasks if the school is to plan the kind of literature program needed to prepare the adults of the twenty-first century.

CURRENT REVIEWING OF CHILDREN'S BOOKS

ZENA SUTHERLAND

THIS paper is designed as an analysis of the current reviewing of children's books and is directed to a question pertinent to the needs of the consumer: "What is the character and the measure of *my* access to current publication of children's literature via the sources of critical evaluation?" I shall examine two studies of current reviewing and report on one of my own, and shall conclude with some comments on what seem to be the unsolved problems, the current needs, any changes or improvements that have come in response to these needs, and a hopeful look at the future.

Two studies of current reviewing have been made, one by Evelyn Anderson in a master's thesis at the University of Chicago and the other by Louise Galloway in a doctoral dissertation at Columbia University. They used somewhat comparable methods, and they concluded with somewhat comparable results. Each analyzed one year of reviewing, giving some attention to policies and practices of their chosen media and scrutinizing in particular those reviews that all of their media had published in common.

First, let us examine Mrs. Anderson's thesis, "A Study of Some Reviewing Media of Children's Books."[1] Based on the recommendations of book selection aids in eight standard publications, Mrs. Anderson chose the following: *Booklist, Bulletin of the Center for Children's Books, Horn Book,* and *School Library*

[1] Evelyn Anderson, "A Study of Some Reviewing Media of Children's Books (unpublished Master's thesis, Graduate Library School, University of Chicago, 1957).

Journal. I shall use that present title of the latter publication; Mrs. Anderson refers to it as *Library Journal* and Miss Galloway as *Junior Libraries*.

The materials analyzed were those reviewed by all four journals out of the list of juvenile books that had been published in 1955, as announced in *Publishers' Weekly*—1,450 titles. Of these, 166 were reviewed by all four journals, the span of publication of these reviews being from July, 1954, to December, 1956. There were 428 books, one-fourth of those published, not reviewed by any of the four journals.

Mrs. Anderson uses a list of fifteen criteria:

1. Length of review
2. Scope
3. Format
4. Illustrations
5. Writing style, literary quality, and treatment
6. Accuracy of material
7. Comparison with other books by the same author or with other books on the same subject
8. Uses—curricular and other
9. Age or grade level
10. Appeals to children's interest
11. Plot development
12. Character development and characterization
13. Rating or indication of outstanding books
14. Weaknesses or limitations
15. Time lag between publication and review

Mrs. Anderson's thesis considers the needs of children's departments in public libraries and the needs of school libraries. She analyzes the reviews of each publication separately, pointing out the strengths and weaknesses she finds in each. The ALA *Booklist* has reviews that are brief but informative

110

about scope; they give a nominal amount of information about format. The reviews appear sooner after publication date than do those of the other three media, and they provide information about the maturity level of each book. *Booklist* is unique in giving pseudonymous names and classification numbers, the latter fact mitigating the minimal amount of suggestions for use. Especially high quality is indicated by inclusion in the list "Suggested for the Small Library."

The *Bulletin* gives reviews that are informative about the scope of the book; it is especially helpful in pointing out special uses; it makes a wide coverage of all children's books published. Reviews are often later in appearing than those of the other three media, and they give a minimal amount of information about format. The *Bulletin* provides information about non-recommended books, gives a maturity level for each book, and uses a helpful coding system for refinement of evaluation.

Mrs. Anderson recognizes mitigating aspects, such as the fact that there may be less need to point out weaknesses of books reviewed in *Horn Book* and the *Booklist*, since all of their books are recommended. She states that the slowness of *Bulletin* reviews is balanced by the fact that that slowness is caused by committee deliberations that produce consistency of reviewing. She concludes that *Booklist* and the *Bulletin* are basic selection tools; *Horn Book* and *School Library Journal* are supplemental.

Miss Galloway, in her dissertation, uses a similar method.[2] She examines, as does Mrs. Anderson, one year of juvenile titles announced in *Publishers' Weekly*—the year 1959, the span of reviewing time for those books extending from January, 1959, to March, 1960. Again, a list of reviewing media was chosen, and the material analyzed was the reviews found in all the journals included in the study. In this case, eight media were examined for the extent of their reviewing and for their usefulness, specifically, as selection aids for school libraries. The eight media are:

1. *Booklist*
2. *Bulletin of the Center for Children's Books*
3. *Horn Book*
4. *School Library Journal*
5. *New York Herald Tribune*
6. *New York Times*
7. *Elementary English*
8. *Saturday Review*

The dissertation discusses reviewing practices, coverage of publication, and the backgrounds of the reviewers. It focuses, however, on an analysis of reviews that appeared in all eight media. In this study there were 126 reviews of 14 books (some having been reviewed more than once out of 1,647 children's trade books published in 1959).

Turning to Miss Galloway's list of criteria we find many that are the same as Mrs. Anderson's.

1. Gist
2. Accuracy
3. Characterization and character development
4. Plot development
5. Treatment of subject
6. Quality and style of writing
7. Special features
8. Typography
9. Paper
10. Binding
11. Page composition

[2] Mabel Louise Galloway, "An Analytical Study of the Extent and Nature of the Reviewing of Juvenile Books in Eight Journals and Newspapers with Special Regard to their Usefulness as Selection Aids for School Libraries" (unpublished Ph.D. dissertation, Teachers College, Columbia University, 1965).

12. Characteristics of illustrations
13. Age or grade level
14. Comparisons with other books by the same author
15. Comparison with other books on the same subject
16. Reader interest to which the book will appeal
17. Curricular or other uses
18. Underlying value
19. Rating

It is important to keep in mind that Miss Galloway includes suggestions for enrichment of curriculum as a necessary aspect of reviews used in book selection for school libraries. She is, therefore, more conscious of comparison with other books on a subject and with other books by the same author than is Mrs. Anderson. Her conclusions differ slightly: She finds *Booklist* reviews of fiction brief or meager, and notes that there is seldom a comment on the qualification of the author and that in none of the reviews is there any comparison to other books on the same subject or other books by the same author.

It seems pertinent to mention here that this comment was made about reviews of only 14 books. The *Bulletin,* she notes, makes almost no mention of the physical features of the books, except for illustrations, and that the reviews contain no comparisons with other books on the same subject or books by the same author. Since the analysis of this study is based on the 14 books considered worth reviewing by eight publications, it is perhaps not surprising that "Most of the reviews that were examined recommended the respective books."

As regards *Horn Book,* Miss Galloway feels that the accounts of the books' contents (the 5 fiction titles) are very general, and the information tends to be quite meager. She says that the reviewers have little to say concerning characterization and character and plot development, but that considerable stress is placed upon communicating the way a subject is treated and the quality and style of writing.

In discussing *School Library Journal,* Miss Galloway remarks that appeals to the reader and uses for the books are often more implied than directly stated; she comments that all 14 books were recommended, and notes that several aspects of the books' physical features are treated in the reviews.

Elementary English reviews Miss Galloway found to be clear and comprehensive for non-fiction, inadequate in making comparisons, and very helpful in suggesting uses. The *New York Herald Tribune* exhibits great variation in length of reviews (from 20 to 900 words). She notes that descriptions of the contents of the 5 fiction books seem more intended to pique one's interest in reading the respective books than to present a clear picture of the wholeness of the story. Again, she points out that there is little information about the physical features of the book and that in only three reviews are there any comparisons with other books on the same subject.

As for the *New York Times,* she comments that the reviewers tend to state the theme of a book rather than to present a clear, whole picture of the contents. In writing about the works of fiction, it is apparent that the reviewers deliberately withhold revealing parts of the plot as though their intent is to whet one's interest in reading the book rather than to impart a full picture of the contents. And, she notes, the appeal to the reader is seldom stated but must be inferred.

Of *Saturday Review,* she notes that

the gist of contents is clearly conveyed and that in all of the reviews the treatment of the subject is stated or implied. None of the reviews specifies an age or grade or grade level; only one review gives the author's qualifications, and none of the reviews includes any comparisons with other books by the same author. This study was made prior to the time Alice Dalgliesh was children's book editor.

Before a note on Miss Galloway's summarizing, it should be stated that the comments above are a skimming of her analysis; she is assiduous in naming the reviewer, in describing the length of reviews, and in giving other facts with careful consistency. The summary states that 73 per cent plus of the 1959 trade books were reviewed by one or more of the journals and newspapers, 26 per cent plus by none, that there is little reviewing prior to publication—indeed, that there is often a considerable time lag—and that only *Booklist* and *School Library Journal* reviewed more than 50 per cent of children's trade books published in 1959. In general, Miss Galloway seems to feel that reviewing—for school library purposes—is inadequate both in quality and in quantity.

Two of Miss Galloway's summary findings merit comment. First, that aside from the *Booklist* and *Horn Book* the reviews include few derogatory criticisms, and in no instance do these criticisms appear to assume sufficient importance to cause the reviewer to reject the book. It seems pertinent to comment that there is a low probability of derogatory criticism, since the reviews were of 14 books out of over 600 published deemed worthy of review by fourteen media.

Second, she comments that the *Bul-letin of the Center for Children's Books* and *Junior Libraries* (*School Library Journal*) consistently use a system of ratings by which they single out books of especial merit. Surely the *Booklist* does this in its list of recommendations for small libraries. Miss Galloway concludes that, since *School Library Journal* and *Booklist* reviewed more than 50 per cent of the 1959 books, they are the two media out of the eight that offer the greatest review coverage for persons choosing juvenile books. Finally, she says, more clearly descriptive and critical reviews are needed that include those aspects of information listed in her criteria; that more space should be given in the present media, or new publications be created.

Although most of this audience is surely familiar with the policies and procedures of *Booklist*, *Bulletin*, *Horn Book*, and *School Library Journal*, it may be useful briefly to review.

The ALA's *Booklist*, which is published every two weeks save for August, is indexed in each issue and the index cumulated twice a year. There are separate sections for children's and for young adult books; the editors choose only books they recommend for purchase. Advisory voting lists are sent out each week for each list to a dozen young people's librarians who, because of their own situation, will have had an opportunity to see the books. Especially recommended books are singled out in the list for small library purchase. A statement of its policy was made in a 1953 issue of *Top of the News* giving the criteria used as a basis of evaluation and stating that the annotations point out shortcomings that may limit the usefulness of the book, and that they make comparisons when possible with other books on the same subject.

The *Bulletin*'s reviews are based on assessments made by the editor and reviewed by a committee of librarians and teachers meeting weekly. To assist librarians who have no opportunity to examine books, in making their selections, non-recommended books are reviewed. The *Bulletin* uses a six-symbol code for evaluation, and the opinions of faculty members who are subject experts are sought when needed. The *Bulletin* is published eleven times a year and indexed annually; the back cover lists professional material each month. In December, a list of titles recommended in the calendar year is included.

Horn Book is published every two months with an index in each issue and annual index. It includes articles and reproductions of illustrations; it reviews only books it recommends, the signed reviews being written by staff members. In addition to regular sections for various age groups, *Horn Book* includes any special heading that may seem useful, even if only one review is given under the special heading. Mrs. Viguers, the editor, said in a meeting reported in the May issue of the 1963 *Library Journal*, "While fortunately libraries do use the *Horn Book* as a help in buying books, we also hope that they make the *Horn Book* available to parents, since it is geared to individuals as well as to library groups wanting recommended books."[3]

At the same meeting, Miss Davis of the *School Library Journal* stated that the main purpose of the publication was "to serve as a buying guide, particularly for average and smaller public and school libraries throughout the country.

Our appraisals are not intended to be definitive literary reviews, nor an attempt to pick out the distinguished books of the year."[4] *School Library Journal* is published monthly from September to May. It is indexed in alternate issues, the books it has recommended during the year being included in a separate annual publication, and it includes articles and professional news; its signed reviews are written by almost a hundred librarians and library supervisors throughout the country. A small panel of librarians serves as advisors for each issue, occasionally deciding on publication of a second review. *School Library Journal* reviews all books it thinks will be seriously considered for purchases by librarians, marking books of special merit with a single or a double asterisk.

It seemed to this investigator fairly apparent that to follow in a third survey the same procedures that were used by Mrs. Anderson and Miss Galloway would produce corroborative evidence —perhaps to the point of monumental redundancy. Clearly, the methods they used—the application of lists of criteria to a comparatively small number of reviews—produced a detailed content analysis but could not give at the same time a broad picture.

In 1965, there were 2,473 juvenile titles published. In examining the reviewing of books in that year, I have chosen not to analyze 1965 titles, but 1965 reviewing. Some of the titles listed in *Publishers' Weekly* in 1965 were, of course, reviewed in 1966, and some of the reviews published in 1965 were reviews of 1964 titles. Since the pattern of time lag repeats each year, there seemed no reason to pursue the 1965 titles.

[3] "Book Reviewer's Summit Conference, the Big Four Speak," *Library Journal*, 88 (May 15, 1963), 2072.

[4] *Ibid.*, p. 2069.

Media used were the *Booklist,* published by the American Library Association; the *Bulletin of the Center for Children's Books,* published by the Graduate Library School of the University of Chicago; *Horn Book Magazine,* published by Horn Book Incorporated, and *School Library Journal,* published by R. R. Bowker Company.

There were 2,299 books reviewed by one or more of the four media. Of these, 1,501 were reviewed by only one publication. The largest number in this category was found in the *School Library Journal*—927 books. Titles reviewed only by the *Bulletin* were 350; *Booklist,* 139; and *Horn Book,* 85. Books reviewed by two of the four media totaled 466; *School Library Journal,* 405; *Booklist,* 203; *Horn Book,* 175; the *Bulletin,* 149.

In the category of books covered by three out of the four media, out of a total of 238, *School Library Journal* covered 211; *Booklist,* 198; *Horn Book,* 176; and the *Bulletin,* 129. Only 94 books out of the total of the 2,299 reviewed were covered by all four of the media. Of the 2,473 titles published in 1965, *School Library Journal* reviewed 1,619; the *Bulletin,* 748; *Booklist,* 608; and *Horn Book,* 530.

One of the problems for most reviewers has been the increasing number of science books—among them, books on fairly technical subjects, or on advanced research, or on the new mathematics with which many of us are unfamiliar. Today, young people are reading books on cryogenics, biochemistry, and computers at a level that would not too long ago have been considered adult material.

Therefore, it is of interest to consider the coverage given science books. It is a low percentage. Out of the 94

books reviewed by all media, only 4 were science titles, a shade over 4 per cent; 12 per cent of the books reviewed by three media were on scientific subjects; 13 per cent of the titles reviewed by two media; and in the case of books covered by only one of the journals, the figure was 12 per cent—the last three very close percentages, all three times as high as the percentage of science books reviewed in the all-four group.

Of the 4 titles in that group, none was in the physical sciences, reflecting the tendency in each group toward a preponderance of reviews of books in the area of the natural sciences.

Another area of interest was the amount of fiction versus non-fiction. Of the books reviewed by one medium only, 721 titles out of 1,501 were non-fiction. Of the 466 titles in the two-media group, 244 were non-fiction. Of the 238 books reviewed in the three-media category, 105 were non-fiction; and there were 28 non-fiction titles in the small group of 94 books reviewed by all four media.

There was unremarkable agreement on reading level. Five reviews each in the *Bulletin* and in the *Booklist* gave levels that differed to any noteworthy degree from those given by the other three media in the 94-book review. *Horn Book* does not give the close definition of reading level as a matter of policy. Although it is difficult to calibrate agreement when the four media assign for one book junior and senior high school, grades 6–9, grades 7–10, and just "Biography," it is possible to say that there still exists, as there did in Mrs. Anderson's study of ten years ago, the highest degree of agreement between *Booklist* and the *Bulletin.*

It is interesting to see that in the list

of 94 books thirty-two publishers are represented—one with 12 books—and eleven publishers with only a single entry. One indication of the publishers' interest in reviewing is the increasing use, in their catalogs, of lists of media whose recommendations of individual titles are noted in a system of coded symbols.

What emerges from this compilation of facts, comparisons, and judgments? No journal gives complete coverage, and no one of the four so intensively scrutinized is without some flaws. There are some constant facts, such as the wide coverage of the *Library Journal* and the personal tone of the *Horn Book*, to which Mrs. Anderson referred as being "characterized by a note of enthusiasm in contrast to the more studied and objective tone of the reviews in the *Booklist* and the *Bulletin of the Children's Book Center*."[5]

There are some differences of opinion: Mrs. Anderson finds that appeals to the reader are usually noted; Miss Galloway does not. I find more comparison with other books on the subject —perhaps this is a developing trend. Mrs. Anderson mentions the fact that, in *Horn Book*, "page references to authors and titles of children's books include advertisements as well as the reviews, with no distinction made in the index as to whether a review or an advertisement is indicated."[6] Advertisers are now indexed separately. The *Bulletin*, once able to review all of the books it received, now receives more of the larger amount published, a fact that has resulted in a larger percentage of recommended books out of its total reviewing.

[5] Anderson, *op. cit.*, p. 46.

[6] *Ibid.*, p. 37.

Most reviewing media have been forced to give up something—series books usually being the first to go. Some media have found that they needed to increase their staffs.

The nature of the inadequacies in current reviewing would indicate that those inadequacies are only partially superable. A co-operative arrangement combined with a proliferation of media for special areas would help. So would governmental or foundation subsidies. Eventually, the computer will come to the help of the librarian selecting books, but that is not imminent.

Examination centers may have increased, but there are still many librarians who have no opportunity to examine new books. Virginia Haviland says, in an article written in 1961,

Small libraries, without approval copies at hand, must usually rely on printed reviews and approved lists and on visits to the bookstores and exhibits. The need for a variety of reviews with their different emphases and coverage is greater for the small library than it is for the larger one with an orderly system of reviewing. There is special help in the "For the Small Library" recommendation in *Booklist;* in the unfavorable as well as favorable verdicts expressed in both *School Library Journal* as well as the *Bulletin of the Center for Children's Books,* with a helpful key also in the latter to "marginal" and "special" values; in the inclusion of illustrations from books and a scientist's reviews in the *Horn Book.*

For the small library, even more important guidance than that of the current reviews (and, says a one-man department, it is "less difficult and time consuming") is that offered later in selective lists and in catalogs with annual supplements, in which entries are starred and double-starred.

ALA's annual "Notable Children's Books" appears each spring; the *Horn Book* "Fanfare" summary is printed in its August issue; during Book Week and before Christmas many lists of the year's outstanding books are printed by large libraries and newspapers. No single summary or review medium is sufficient, but a number of them together become a substitute for reading and examination of the books themselves.[7]

Virginia Haviland also mentions the system of comparative reviewing that was used by librarians of greater Boston. Part of current reviewing practice is certainly a lively exchange of opinion. At the Children's Services Division meeting in New York, a panel of three editors and three reviewers discussed policies and books. The questions from the floor made it clear that CSD members were anxious to talk about "controversial" books. With the advent of books like *Harriet the Spy* and *Dorp Dead,* there has been sounded an acid note in exchanges of opinion—a note some find moderately distressing. These books seem to be a reflection of our literary times, perhaps a reflection in juvenile literature of Salinger and Kerouac. We do not need to agree on the merit of a book, but in making acid comments about a conflicting opinion we are indulging in internecine pyrotechnics that are less than instructive or dignified.

It is also apparent that there is need for clarification of the terms we use, both in evaluations of books and in descriptions of books and their audiences.

Perhaps the "controversial" or "trend" books are overanalyzed; so, perhaps, are the beginner books. Let's face it: some of them are delightful, some of them are deadly dull, and the rest—which is the largest number—vary from innocuous mediocrity to pedestrian usefulness that verges on textbook sterility.

There are so many books published; how does a reviewing journal decide what to include and what to omit?

[7] Virginia Haviland, "Search for the Real Thing," *Library Journal,* **86** (December 15, 1961), 4334.

Clearly, for some users, the journal that reviews non-recommended books serves a need. For some, the reviews of only recommended books is sufficient. Certainly a librarian, or a teacher, or a parent who is selecting books should ideally use all of the media available and should also, ideally, know the policies and the tone of each publication he uses and be aware of the special values or the limitations of each.

The user must also evaluate the medium in terms of its intended audience. The tendency in newspapers and some magazines to describe 2 or more books in a comparative review seems perfectly acceptable for its audience of individual subscribers. They do not need the decimal classification of *Booklist;* librarians do. They do not want *School Library Journal*'s information on binding; librarians do. Young parents need to be reminded of old books; young librarians are likely to have the old books and be stunned by the spate of new books. They need information and critical evaluation and some discussion.

There are readers for all books of merit. In a meeting of the New York State Library Association at which four reviewers spoke and conducted a question period, a librarian asked, "Why does the Newbery-Caldecott Committee pick Newbery Award winners that sit on the shelves and just don't circulate?" Mrs. Viguers volunteered a succinct answer to the effect that we surely want Shakespeare in every library even though not everybody enjoys Shakespeare.

The problem of the reviewer's audience was also touched upon by some booksellers during a recent ALA Conference. The booksellers collect reviews and take them along on their trips, but often discover that the librarian or supervisor is not interested and prefers the salesman to select the books. To these men, there were two problems in reviewing; one, that reviews were not objective enough; two, that they failed to consider the wide disparity in levels of sophistication and reading ability in different geographical areas. It seems difficult to solve the latter problem. One can hardly grade a book 4–6 with a note that it should be used in primary grades in backward areas.

This is one of the things the user of reviews must judge. The reader should know the consistent practices of the media he uses. And reviewers must avoid the pitfall of assumptions. Let me give two examples. These are comments from reviews in a sample of a proposed new paperback review service.

Speaking of Arthur Goldberg and his career: "Thus when he writes a history of the labor organization it can be viewed as a definitive work." And this: "The account starts when the author was ten years of age, so its appeal to a young reader is assured."

Today the need for reviews seems greater than ever. There are more books, there are more libraries, and there has been loosed an abundance of money. Circulation figures have risen sharply. Between 1960 and 1965, *Booklist* circulation rose 45 per cent. Helen Kinsey, editor of the "Children's Books" section, says that over half the subscribers are now school libraries. Mrs. Viguers reports a tripling of *Horn Book* subsciptions in the past eight years, and the increase has been approximately the same for the *Bulletin*.

Hilary Deason said that to his surprise and pleasure the new quarterly review, *Science Books,* had reached a circulation of 5,000 in its first year.

The Detroit Public Library has announced that its list of books, published monthly, is now available to subscribers and will include two lists, "Books Approved for Purchase," and "Considered but not Included." The *Virginia Kirkus Service* is a hardy perennial, and *Young Readers' Review* is growing nicely. The regular or special-issue reviews in educational journals and science magazines are more and more mentioned in lists of review media. And there is a flourishing proliferation of the bibliographies and selected lists mentioned by Miss Haviland—including her own list, *Children's Books 1965.*[8]

It seems reasonable to conclude that 1967 will bring as many new books for children and young people as did 1965 and 1966, and that most of these books will have some review coverage. Probably there will be relatively few books reviewed in many media, and those few will be books of good quality that merit, but do not need, comparative assessments. Possibly the need for such assessments will lead either to co-operative reviewing or to some practical division of responsibilities; certainly this need will eventually be met in part by the acceleration that will be gained by using such mechanized processes as the future will bring.

[8] Virginia Haviland and Lois B. Watt, *Children's Books 1965* (Washington: U.S. Government Printing Office, 1966).

THE CRITIC AND CHILDREN'S LITERATURE

ELIZABETH NESBITT

BEFORE entering upon a discussion of the relationship between the critic and children's literature, it is desirable to decide what a critic is and what he does. *Webster's New Collegiate Dictionary*[1] defines a critic as one "who expresses a reasoned opinion on any matter, involving a judgment of its values, truth, or righteousness or an appreciation of its beauty and technique." More specifically, the dictionary says that a "critic is skilled in judging the merits of literary and artistic works." Matthew Arnold's definition of the act of criticism is "a disinterested endeavor to learn and propagate the best that is known throughout the world."[2]

These definitions will bear analysis of important implications. Webster's "reasoned opinion" and Arnold's "disinterested endeavor" by inference say that the exclusively personal response, the uninformed, unsubstantiated, impulsive opinion, the preconceived idea, the biased attitude do not result in valid criticism. The dictionary and Arnold also agree that criticism involves judgment in the identification of what is best and of why it is the best. Arnold further intimates that the ability to recognize the best is the result of a learning process, and it is obvious that this learning comprises a knowledge, wide and discriminating, of the best of the past and the present. Arnold indi-

cates that the critic does not stop with his own recognition of quality. His joy of discovery of the best is such that he has the desire to persuade others to share with him the delight of this discovery and that he feels the desire to give permanence to that which is truly great.

There is a distinction between literary criticism and book-reviewing which should be made clear. The introduction to *English Critical Essays, Twentieth Century* says, "Reviewing may or may not be criticism"[3] and warns against the tacit assumption that reviewing is necessarily and always literary criticism, though it sometimes may be. Helen Haines, in *What's in a Novel*, goes into greater detail on this point.

Two principles dominate virtually all book reviewing. One is the principle set forth by Anatole France, when he defined criticism as "the adventures of the soul among the masterpieces of literature." This is essentially the principle of the literary and critical essay, not of the book review. It interprets in terms of intellectual or emotional analysis; it may convey a work in part rather than as a whole; and it follows no conventionalized form of organization or treatment. The second principle represents an impersonal (or as impersonal as possible) consideration of an author's work. This is essentially the principle of the book review, as a logically organized summary and appraisal of a book as a whole. And in the field of book reviewing, Anatole France has been responsible for sad havoc. The adventures of a reviewer's soul may be edifying, illuminating, entertaining. When they record the conclusions of an expert critic, a literary artist, they invigorate and enrich the study of liter-

[1] 2d ed.; Springfield, Mass.: G. & C. Merriam Co., 1949, p. 197.

[2] Matthew Arnold, "The Function of Criticism," *Lectures and Essays in Criticism* (Ann Arbor: University of Michigan Press, 1962), p. 283.

[3] Phyllis M. Jones (ed.), *English Critical Essays, Twentieth Century* (London: Oxford University Press, 1933), p. x.

ature, but in their more ordinary manifestations they give us, in sum, a review of the reviewer in his personal relation to a given book rather than a review of the book itself. Impersonal consideration of an author's work, on the other hand, is founded on a familiar dictum: a reviewer should tell what the author set out to do, what he did and how he did it. This remains, I think, the basic principle of good reviewing.[4]

Dr. Richard Darling, in his doctoral dissertation, "Reviewing of Children's Books in American Periodicals, 1865–1881," makes a comparable distinction between literary criticism and reviewing, saying that "most writers agree that a review is a part of journalism, rather than a part of literature, or of literary criticism proper."[5] The years 1865–81 were chosen by Darling in part to correct the misconception that serious criticism of children's books did not appear until nearly the end of the second decade of the twentieth century, as was mistakenly stated in *A Critical History of Children's Literature.*[6] He also calls attention to the fact that in 1883 Caroline M. Hewins began compiling annually for *The Library Journal* a kind of anthology of reviews of children's books. No such record exists for preceding years, but Darling's detailed examination of thirty-six periodicals in publication between 1865 and 1881 gives ample evidence of the extent of reviewing of children's books during this period. It also testifies to the wide variety of magazines that published such re

views—magazines, such as *The Literary World, The Dial, The Critic,* and *The Nation,* that concentrated on the reviewing of books, literary monthlies, such as *The Atlantic Monthly, Scribner's Monthly, Harper's New Monthly Magazine,* children's magazines, notably *The Riverside Magazine* and *St. Nicholas,* and religious and educational periodicals. His chapter called "Reviewing of Selected Books"—in which he brings together and discusses reviews of such books as *Hans Brinker, Little Women, Alice's Adventures in Wonderland, Through the Looking-Glass, The Adventures of Tom Sawyer,* and *The Prince and the Pauper*—substantiates his claim that not only was this reviewing plentiful but much of it had quality, conforming to the principles that should govern book-reviewing. It also showed itself receptive to new trends, and it had respect for children's literature as literature. There were reviews that were inadequate or that misdirected their criticisms, but no age has been free of such. These years also produced literary criticism in relation to children's books, in the editorial writing of Horace E. Scudder in *The Riverside Magazine.*

There was reason for the existence of such criticism at this particular time. The latter half of the nineteenth century and the first ten years of the twentieth century have been said to constitute a golden age of children's literature in England and America, because of the excellence of many of the books written during these years. It is not accidental that this period should also be the one in which interest in and recognition of the literary worth existent in children's books were manifested in general articles, reviews, and selective lists of children's books, such as

[4] Helen Haines, *What's in a Novel* (New York: Columbia University Press, 1942), p. 241.

[5] Richard L. Darling, "Reviewing of Children's Books in American Periodicals, 1865–1881" (unpublished Ph.D. dissertation, University of Michigan, 1960), p. 96.

[6] Cornelia Meigs *et al., A Critical History of Children's Literature* (New York: Macmillan Co., 1953), pp. 421–22.

Caroline M. Hewins' *Books for the Young,* published in 1882.

Neither the creation of a body of genuine literature for children nor the emergence of an equally important body of criticism dealing with this literature was as sudden or accidental as either might seem to be. As Darling says, this was a period when periodicals flourished and when they were of importance in the development in America of literature and of the art of illustration as well. It was natural that these same magazines should turn to the criticism of literature. The simultaneity of the appearance of better writing for children and of criticism of this writing was not fortuitous or unrelated. There was change in the air, excitement in the new freedom and liberality obtained when writers threw off the shackles of prescribed rules regarding form and content; when the former belief that literature for the young must serve only moralistic or utilitarian purposes was recognized as the prohibitive thing it is; when the new idea that literature may exist for the purpose of giving pleasure and delight alone freed the minds and imaginations of writers. These changes, these new beliefs, had their roots in other, and for the time, revolutionary ways of thinking. The former conception of the child as a miniature adult changed to a conception of the child as an individual in his own right, and childhood came to be looked upon as a way of life. As one consequence, there came a waning of the long-lasting and hitherto dominant Puritanic and didactic influences which had for too long a time been the chief motivations in writing for children. Parenthetically and regretfully, it must be admitted that these influences have never completely vanished and that one

of the obligations of contemporary criticism should be to learn from the past and to apply the lesson to the present. Perspective makes us clear sighted and frequently scornful as to the faults of previous centuries; lack of perspective makes us less clear sighted as to comparable faults in our own century. The new spirit in the creation of literature, children's and adult, spread into the field of criticism.

Creative literature has, in the past, and should in the present call forth creative criticism, and this should be as true of children's literature as of adult. Criticism may manifest itself in various forms. In the form of the book review, it should serve a utilitarian as well as a stimulating purpose. In this form, it must deal not only with the truly great but also with the near great and with that which misses greatness altogether. And always, with whatever it may be concerned, it must establish, with clarity, preciseness, and enlightenment, the quality or lack of quality of the writing in question. If criticism is to have the effect upon children's literature that it should have, that is, the effect of convinced acceptance of children's literature as an integral and significant part of the total body of literature of any country, then it must not only, in Arnold's words, "learn to know and propagate the best," it must also learn to know and discourage the worst. Of equal importance is the discernment of positive versus negative qualities in a book, the pinpointing of the positive and the negative, and the relationship between them. For it is true that a book may have weaknesses but may at the same time accomplish something so positive, so worthwhile, so constructive as to negative its faults.

Although there is an admitted distinction between book-reviewing and literary criticism, the same basic principles of criticism underlie both exemplifications of the art of criticism. The reviewer and the literary critic should both possess certain qualities. It goes without saying that both should have a personal, long-standing, and catholic acquaintance with all literature, past and present, adult and children's. This alone is not enough. They must have discerning judgment, a quick and ever fresh responsiveness disciplined by constructively critical minds, the ability to deal in words with the elusive intangibles that make for greatness in art of any kind, and the ability to recreate the image of the work with which they are concerned. If this sounds too formidable for credibility, it is well to re-emphasize that, if the relationship between criticism and children's literature is such as to accomplish the desired result of maintaining the prestige of children's literature as literature, nothing less is acceptable. Written criticism, whether in the form of the general article or the review of a specific book, should be in the hands of people of these prescribed attainments. Even the more remote form of criticism exercised in the selection of children's books for any purpose, whether that purpose be publication, the compiling of a selective bibliography, or the building of a book collection, should be in the hands of those thoroughly versed in the fundamental principles of criticism and in the use of books with children.

The critical sense and even the facility in expression of the results of the critical sense may be cultivated. They must be, if we are to get the quantity and quality of criticism of children's books we need. It is a temptation to say that all who are concerned professionally with children's books should be required to take courses in the history of literary criticism and in the performance of criticism. Since this will undoubtedly be judged impractical, the next best thing, and no mean substitute, is the reading of the critical essayists. Not only do they afford reading fascinating in itself, the enlightenment provided by their insight into the heart of greatness and by their expression of that insight is frequently literally dazzling, because, as Miss Haines says, the principle of the literary and critical essay is interpretative, and interpretative in terms of intellectual or emotional analysis. And it is surprising to discover that at least occasionally what they have to say bears directly or indirectly on the matter of critical judgment of children's books and reading. The writings of such critics as Matthew Arnold, William Hazlitt, J. Middleton Murry, Robert Louis Stevenson, Edmund Gosse, George Saintsbury, and others, repay a thousand times every minute spent with them.

Detailed reference to one such essay is justified because it is, for the theme with which it deals, an excellent exposition of certain reading tastes of children and of what the books that satisfy these tastes should be. It was, of course, not intended to be such. Robert Louis Stevenson's *A Gossip on Romance* is worth study for the excellence of its construction alone. Apart from this, Stevenson has written here something that throws light on some of the perplexing problems of criticism of children's books, particularly the problem of the difference between the immoral and amoral. The following quotation begins with one of those sentences of startling import frequently found in these essays. "Drama is the poetry of conduct, romance the poetry of circumstance . . . There is a vast deal in life and letters both which is not immoral, but simply amoral . . . where the interest turns, not upon what a man shall choose to do, but on how he manages to do it; not on the passionate slips and hesitations of the conscience, but on the problems of the body and of the practical intelligence, in clean, open-air adventure, the shock of arms or the diplomacy of life."[7] Surely this passage explains the classic adventure quality of *Treasure Island*. A clear understanding of the meaning of the passage would as certainly render our criticism of adventure less confused, more intelligent, and more just. Indeed, one of the most important realizations conveyed by this essay is the realization that each kind of literature has its own peculiar requirements and that these requirements must be established and a book judged in accordance with its fulfilment of these requirements.

Over and over again, Stevenson emphasizes the need in adventure, or, as he calls it, "romance," for "fit and striking incident," and we know that children read for incident. He says:

The right kind of thing should fall out in the right kind of place, the right kind of thing should follow; . . . all the circumstances in a tale [should] answer one to another like notes in music. The threads of a story come from time to time together and make a picture in the web; the characters fall from time to time into some attitude to each other or to nature which stamps the story home like an illustration. Crusoe recoiling from the foot-print, Achilles shouting over against the Trojans, Ulysses bending the great bow, Christian running with his fingers in his ears, these are each culminating moments in the legend, and each has been printed on the mind's eye forever . . . This is the highest and the hardest thing to do in words; the thing, which once accomplished, equally delights the schoolboy and the sage, and makes, in its own right, the quality of epics . . . It is one thing . . . to describe scenery with the word painters; it is quite another thing to seize on the heart of the suggestion and make a country famous with a legend. It is one thing to dissect, with the most cutting logic, the complications of life, and of the human spirit; it is quite another to give them body and blood in the story of Ajax or of Hamlet. The first is literature, but the second is something besides, for it is likewise art.[8]

The impact of that is tremendous and grows with every rereading. It defines, with accuracy so sharp as to be startling, the central greatness of much literature, from the epics to modern writings. *Johnny Tremain*, by Esther Forbes, has in it many praiseworthy things, but its chief claim to distinction lies in one culminating moment, when the whole meaning of the book, of the American Revolution and of all similar struggles, is laid bare, the moment when James Otis says, "We fight, we die, for a simple thing, that a man may stand up." A penetrating and experienced critic might see this without the help of Stevenson's essay, but most of us need a pointing of the way, such as is afforded by Stevenson and other essayists. A critic should be aware that this moment in *Johnny Tremain* is one of those culminating moments that has been printed on the eye's mind forever and that it is chiefly, though not entirely, this moment that gives the book distinction.

[7] Robert Louis Stevenson, "A Gossip on Romance," in George Scott-Moncrieff (ed.), *Selected Essays, Robert Louis Stevenson* (Chicago: Henry Regnery Co., 1959), p. 246.

[8] *Ibid.*, pp. 249–51.

Another case in point is Matthew Arnold's expert analysis of the Celtic genius contained in his essay "On the Study of Celtic Literature."[9] His description of the unique flavor imparted to any literature touched by the Celtic spirit has intense value for any who are in any way dealing with such literature, retellers of tales, selectors and critics of these retellings, and story tellers who may be using the retellings.

Formal or informal study of written criticisms such as those cited will help to give contemporary book reviewers and literary critics the necessary sound grasp of fundamental critical principles needed for evaluation of the flood of children's books published today. Since these books show great variety of kind, critics should be able to define clearly the requirements of each form of literature and to establish with equal clarity whether or not the book in question lives up to these requirements. A fine example of the effectiveness of this kind of review is afforded by William Soskin's review of Geoffrey Household's *Rogue Male*, published many years ago in the *Herald Tribune Books*.

A novel of this sort requires very definite qualities of story telling. Its writing must first of all create a shadowy atmosphere, a twilight in which the animal instincts, the almost lurid melodrama of the chase, the fearful tension and the sheer factual basis of the drama may all be merged in a reality all their own. Beyond that, it must, if it is not to be merely a hackneyed compounding of the ingredients of adventure, stress subtleties of character and of its people's mental processes. It must contain implications—in this case, of the social effects of dictatorships and modern foreign office methods—beyond the factual content of the story, and it must not suggest these overtones in any blatant or gauche fashion.[10]

Mr. Soskin goes on to demonstrate with exactness that the book he is reviewing fully meets these necessities. It is true that this kind of review demands more space than is frequently allotted to reviews of children's books. But justice to important books for children and to the reviewers who deal with them means that those books that are in any way significant deserve something more than a notice or a critical annotation and should be treated as comparable adult books would be treated.

Webster's New Collegiate Dictionary gives a third and derogatory definition of a critic, "one given to harsh or captious judgment; a caviler or carper."[11] A competent critic does not approach the critical reading of a book with the preconceived intention of finding in it things that may be destructively criticized, with the hope that on page so-and-so he may find language, incidents, details, attitudes to which he may object, thereby proving to himself, and hopefully only to himself, that he is critical. So he is, but in the petty, carping sense of the word. The competent critic, when he does find something deserving of adverse criticism, does not draw it completely out of context, thereby exaggerating it out of proportion. Also, if he is competent, he has a sense of the fitness of things, a realization that the true test of style is fitness of form and expression to thought and nature of content. It is one thing to analyze and dissect a book, so that at last it lies in disjointed, heterogeneous fragments. It is another thing to rebuild

[9] Arnold, *op. cit.*, pp. 291–386.

[10] William Soskin, *"Rogue Male,* by Geoffrey Household" [Review], *New York Herald Tribune*, Sec. IX, *Books* (August 27, 1939), p. 4.

[11] *Op. cit.*

from these fragments the whole of a book; to paraphrase Stevenson, it is another thing to give a book body and blood. But it is essential that any critical comment leave the reader or listener with a totality of impression, because otherwise less than justice has been done to a book, even to those that may miss greatness.

It follows that a good critic must have the sense of selectivity that leads to the stressing of essentials and the lesser consideration of trivialities and banalities. He must view criticism as positive and constructive, rather than negative and destructive. He must have the ability to recreate, in his criticism, the spirit and essence, not merely the plot or content, of the literature with which he is dealing. He must have not only knowledge of the reading interests and preferences of children but also faith in the child's potential responsiveness to genuine greatness.

This last sentence calls to attention the fact that the comment so far has been directed chiefly toward criticism's obligation to identify literature and non-literature and to document the identification. Only passing mention has been made of the admittedly necessary consideration of children's needs, interests, and desires, and no mention has been made of the evaluation of subject-matter books. The emphasis has been placed, in this paper, on the point that seems, to me, to need primary consideration at this time. There may be, reasonably, difference of opinion in this respect.

The question arises, how may critics of the kind described be developed? And the immediate answer is that too little attention has been paid to the development of the fine art of criticism in relation to children's literature. Potential critical ability in students, writers, librarians, or any other persons should be recognized and nourished. Special interests in specific fields of literature, for example poetry, fantasy, folk literature, biography, should be encouraged and allowed to expand, so that these people become authoritative within their fields of interest, thereby providing specialists in criticism whose extent of knowledge will give their criticism authority and whose informed appreciation, interest and enthusiasm will give their criticism vitality. Critical study of criticism, past and present, should be a part of every course in children's literature, as it may be of some. Indeed, it might be well worth while to incorporate courses dealing with the study and performance of criticism, courses that would carry the consideration of criticism beyond the usual requirements of written critical annotations and of written and oral book reviews.

From the beginning, children's books have been reflective of the periods in which they were written. From the 1860's on, there have been children's books that are the creations of great minds, of great imaginations, and of the comparatively rare qualities of compassion and of the awareness of the mystery of the struggle of humankind for truth and for the secret of human destiny; books that are replete with the thing Sir Arthur Quiller-Couch was talking about when he said, in his book *On the Art of Reading,* "I preach to you that the base of all literature, of all poetry, of all theology, is one, and stands on one rock; the very highest universal truth is something so simple that a child may understand it.[12] It is the existence of children's books of this kind that leads me to put in a personal plea, not for fewer book reviews, but for more articles of literary criticism. These do appear from time to time, and their very location in whatever publication they appear is of significance, since they are usually not associated with the pages on which reviews of children's books appear in the periodicals devoted to consideration of literature; or they appear in general periodicals devoted to adult interests. The signifi-

[12] New York: G. P. Putnam's Sons, 1920, p. 68.

cance lies in the tacit acknowledgment that the literature with which the articles are concerned escapes limitations of age or any other barrier, that it is of such import that it is a part of the imperishable literature of the world.

Criticism of the right kind, in whatever form it may take, may and should serve several purposes, informational, evaluative, and stimulative. It should be drawn into being by the existence of literature worthy of serious, intelligent, and even inspired criticism. In turn, such criticism encourages, stimulates, and rewards literature worthy of criticism's best efforts.

THE CONTRIBUTORS

MARIAN EDMAN: professor, Wayne State University. Born St. Paul, Minnesota, 1901. B.A., Gustavus Adolphus College, 1926; M.A. (1935), Ph.D. (1938), University of Minnesota. From 1928 to 1932, instructor, Gustavus Adolphus College. From 1937 to 1938, librarian, Laboratory School, University of Chicago. Summer guest lecturer: Universities of Minnesota, Chicago, California, Ohio State, West Virginia, Michigan, and Western Michigan. Also teacher education specialist, Department of State, in Germany, Lebanon, and Viet Nam. Member National Council of Teachers of English, Association for Childhood Education, Association for Student Teaching, and Pi Lambda Theta. Publications: *Invitation to Reading* (New York: Harcourt, Brace & Co., 1942), *Reading for Enjoyment* (Boston: Houghton Mifflin Co., 1955), *Horizon of Man* (Detroit: Wayne State University Press, 1963), and *Cross Cultural Study of the Primary Teacher* (Detroit: Wayne State University Press, 1966).

SARA INNIS FENWICK: associate professor, University of Chicago, and supervising editor, *Bulletin of the Center for Children's Books*. Born Lima, Ohio. B.A., Western Reserve University; M.A., Graduate Library School, University of Chicago. From 1931 to 1944, assistant children's librarian, young people's librarian, and head of work with children, Wilkes-Barre, Pennsylvania, Public Library. From 1944 to 1946, assistant to director of work with children, Enoch Pratt Free Library, Baltimore, Maryland. From 1946 to 1949, head of work with children, Gary, Indiana, Public Library. From 1949 to 1956, elementary school librarian, Laboratory School, University of Chicago. Also summer school visiting lecturer and instructor in Extension Center, Indiana University. Member of American Library Association, International Reading Association, National Education Association, Association for Higher Education, Department of Audiovisual Instruction, Association for Supervision and Curriculum Development, Illinois Education Association,

Illinois Library Association, Pi Lambda Theta, Delta Kappa Gamma, National Council of Teachers of English, and American Association of School Librarians. NEA delegate to World Confederation of Organizations of the Teaching Profession, 1963. Fulbright senior lecturer to Australia, 1964. Author of articles in professional journals and monographs and *School and Children's Libraries in Australia* (Melbourne: F. W. Cheshire, 1966); edited *New Definitions of School Library Service*, Proceedings of the Annual Conference of the Graduate Library School, 1959 (Chicago: University of Chicago Press, 1960).

KATHARINE H. KAPPAS: occupational therapist, Washington, D.C. Born Evanston, Illinois, 1930. B.A., Vassar College, 1952; M.A., University of Chicago, 1965. 1955–56, children's librarian, Chicago Public Library. Editor, Follett Publishing Company, Chicago. Member, American Library Association.

DAVID MCCORD: poet. Born New York City, 1897. A.B. (1921), A.M. (1922), Harvard. From 1923 to 1928, drama and music staff, *Boston Evening Transcript*. From 1925 to 1963, executive director, Harvard Fund Council. From 1940 to 1946, editor, *Harvard Alumni Bulletin*.

Honors: Phi Beta Kappa; Phi Beta Kappa poet at Harvard, Tufts, and The College of William and Mary; Lowell Lectures, Boston, 1950; Guggenheim Fellow, 1954; Honorary Curator of Poetry and Farnsworth Rooms, Harvard College Library; L.H.D., Harvard, 1956; Sarah Josepha Hale Medal, 1962. Exhibition, Boston Public Library, November 10–December 10, 1966, of his writings, drawings, and water colors.

Associations: Trustee, Boston Athenaeum; Fellow, American Academy of Arts and Sciences; Colonial Society of Massachusetts; Massachusetts Historial Society.

Publications: written and edited 30 books of poetry and essays. Three recent books of poetry for children include *Far and Few* (Boston: Little, Brown & Co., 1952), *Take Sky*

(Boston: Little, Brown & Co., 1963), and *All Day Long* (Boston: Little, Brown & Co., 1966).

ELIZABETH NESBITT: associate dean, Carnegie Library School (1948–62). Born Northumberland, Pennsylvania, 1897. B.A., Goucher College, 1918; B.S. in L.S., Carnegie Institute of Technology, 1922; M.A., University of Pittsburgh, 1932. From 1922 to 1924, children's librarian, Carnegie Library, Pittsburgh; 1924 to 1926, supervisor of story telling. From 1926 to 1929, librarian, Clarion State Teachers College, Pennsylvania. From 1929 to 1945, assistant professor, Carnegie Library School. From 1945 to 1948, head, Boys and Girls Department, Carnegie Library, Pittsburgh. Author of *Howard Pyle* (New York: Henry Z. Walck, Inc., 1966); co-author of *A Critical History of Children's Literature* (New York: Macmillan Co., 1953).

EMILY CHENEY NEVILLE: novelist. Born Manchester, Connecticut, 1919. A.B., Bryn Mawr, 1940. From 1941 to 1942, feature writer for *New York Mirror*. Author of *It's Like This, Cat* (New York: Newbery Award, Harper & Row, 1963), *Berries Goodman* (New York: Harper & Row, 1965), and *The Seventeenth Street Gang* (New York: Harper & Row, 1966).

EDWARD W. ROSENHEIM, JR.: professor, University of Chicago. Born Chicago, Illinois, 1918. B.A. (1939), M.A. (1946), and Ph.D. with honors (1953), University of Chicago. From 1941 to 1946, captain, Infantry, U.S. Army. 1946, instructor, Gary College. Instructor (1947–51), assistant professor (1951–56), associate professor (1956–61), University of Chicago. Member Modern Language Association, National Council of Teachers of English, Johnsonian Society of the Central Region. Publications include *What Happens in Literature* (Chicago: University of Chicago Press, 1960), *Swift and the Satirist's Art* (Chicago: University of Chicago Press, 1963), and editor of *Selected Prose and Poetry of Jonathan Swift* (New York: Holt, Rinehart & Winston, 1959).

JACQUELYN SANDERS: fellow at U.C.L.A. continuing work toward a Ph.D. in education. Born Boston, Massachusetts, 1931. B.A.,

Radcliffe College, 1952; M.A., University of Chicago, 1964; graduate work, University of Chicago, 1964–65. From 1952 to 1963, counselor, Orthogenic School, University of Chicago; assistant principal, 1964–65. 1965, consultant, Osawatomie State Hospital. Spring 1966, postgraduate research educationist, developing instructional material for preschool culturally deprived children, U.C.L.A. Member, Pi Lambda Theta and American Educational Research Association.

H. JOSEPH SCHWARCZ: teacher of education in Teachers' College, Oranim, Israel. Born Vienna, Austria, 1917. Undergraduate work, University, Vienna, and Teachers' College, Jerusalem; M.A., University of Chicago. Former teacher in elementary and secondary schools. Publications include various papers on pedagogical and psychological subjects in Israeli periodicals.

MILLICENT SELSAM: biology teacher, New York City high schools. Born New York City, 1912. B.A., Brooklyn College; M.A. and course work for Ph.D., Columbia University. Author of 37 books about science for children, including *Birth of an Island* (New York: Harper & Bros., 1959), *How Animals Live Together* (New York: William Morrow & Co., 1963), and *Language of Animals* (New York: William Morrow & Co., 1962). Edited *Voyage of the Beagle* by Charles Darwin (New York: Harper & Bros., 1959).

ZENA SUTHERLAND: editor, *Bulletin of the Center for Children's Books*, University of Chicago, 1957 to present, and editor of books for young people, *Saturday Review*. Born Winthrop, Massachusetts, 1915. B.A., University of Chicago, 1937. Member, American Library Association and National Council of Teachers of English.

LUITGARD WUNDHEILER: Born Marburg/Lahn, Germany, 1922. M.A. and Ph.D. degrees, University of Marburg, 1946. From 1955 to 1959, teacher, Laboratory School, University of Chicago. From 1961 to 1965, teacher and therapist, Orthogenic School, University of Chicago. Publications include essays about fairy tales by Goethe and Novalis published by Scherpe-Verlag, Krefeld.

DORIS YOUNG: Born Decatur, Iowa, 1920. B.S., Drake University, 1947; M.A. (1952) and Ph.D. (1956), Northwestern University. From 1939 to 1956, elementary teacher in Milo, Lamoni, and Council Bluffs, Iowa, and Glencoe and Skokie, Illinois. From 1952 to 1954, instructor, Northwestern University. From 1956 to 1958, assistant professor, Michigan State University. From 1958 to 1964, associate professor, Purdue University. Member, American Education Research Association, Association for Supervision and Curriculum Development, National Science Teachers Association, National Council of Teachers of English, National Society for the Study of Education, and American Library Association. Publications include numerous articles for educational journals and yearbooks.